MISSISSIPPI COUNTY, ARKANSAS

DEFINING THE EASTERN BORDER OF ARKANSAS is not as simple as you would think. Yes, the Mississippi River defines the eastern border… well, yes and no. In 1833, when the boundary was drawn between Mississippi County, Arkansas, and Tennessee, mistakes were made due to poor surveying equipment. Then, to add to the confusion, in 1915 when the sheriff of Mississippi County was killed by bootleggers on Island 37 (also known as Devil's Elbow, about thirty-five miles north of Memphis) a dispute arose between Arkansas and Tennessee. It was then discovered that over the years the river had actually moved a bit in places; therefore, Tennessee's boundary with Arkansas today lies where we think the channel of the river was in 1836 when Arkansas became a state. It took the Supreme Court of the United States to figure this out.

The map of Mississippi County, Arkansas, on the opposite page is drawn by me from a combination of older and recent maps of Arkansas. The lettering is by Kristin Muzzarelli.

FIELDS OF WHITE GOLD

Remembering a Forgotten Time
in the Arkansas Delta

GEORGE ANN BYRD DANEHOWER

FIELDS OF WHITE GOLD
Remembering a Forgotten Time in the Arkansas Delta
by George Ann Byrd Danehower

Copyright © 2019 by George Ann Byrd Danehower
Cover and interior art © 2019 by ISz

Published by ACTA Publications, 4848 N. Clark Street,
Chicago, IL 60640, (800) 397-2282, www.actapublications.com

All rights reserved. No part of this publication may be reproduced or transmitted in any form or by any means, electronic or mechanical, including photocopying and recording, or by any information storage and retrieval system, including the Internet, without permission from the publisher. Permission is hereby given to use short excerpts with proper citation in reviews and marketing copy, church bulletins and handouts, and scholarly papers.

Library of Congress Number: 2019914237
ISBN: 978-0-87946-970-2
Printed in the United States of America by Total Printing Systems
Year 30 29 28 27 26 25 24 23 22 21 20
Printing 20 19 18 17 16 15 14 13 12 11 10 9 8 7 6 5 4 3 2

CONTENTS

PREFACE 1
INTRODUCTION 3

THE STORIES
The Mushroom House and the Cotton Fields 9
The Store: Wood and Brick 17
Driving, Cigarettes, and Guns... 23
The Medicine Man, the Witch the TB Lady, and Tight 27
Candy, followed by Books and a Bridge 35
Chuck Wagon and an Angel 39
The George Ann Theater 43
Thief and Murderer 47
The Cotton Gin, Hide and Seek,
    and Spontaneous Combustion 51
Holy Rollers, followed by Soft Cream,
    and a Picture Show 55
Into the River and Bug Funerals... 61
Cousins: Tennessee, Arkansas, Mississippi 67
The First Day of My First 1st Grade 77
The Big Move... 83
The First Day of My Second 1st Grade 91
The Test, the Worm, and Paralysis...................................... 95
The Biggest Worry of All 103

Easter, 4th of July, and Thanksgiving.................................109
Main Street, Parades, and Church Nativity Scene................119
Christmas at Home and in School...................................127
Christmas at the Store, in Florida,
    and over Family Dinners..133
Vision of the End 141
The Blues, Bladie Madie, and the Lord.............................147
The Weirdest Tale of All...157

APPENDICES
The Ditches...163
The Indian Mound...169
The Blues 173
The (infamous) $100.00 Cake Recipe
    From Opal Woods and the Waldorf Astoria...................177
Two Famous Opposites from Mississippi County 179

ACKNOWLEDGMENTS 181

ABOUT THE AUTHOR AND THE ARTIST 183

DEDICATED

to the Memory of
Daddy (George I. Byrd) and Mother (Donye Edwards Byrd),
Papa and Mama Edwards,
and the hard-working people of Mandalay
during the "hard years," 1930-1950

PREFACE

THE SHORT STORIES YOU ARE ABOUT TO READ are true events that were securely stored in my memory many years ago. I had loving parents, whom I called "Daddy" and "Mother," but they were extremely busy parents, so I had freedom unlike most children. In some ways, in fact, I raised myself. Living in a house connected to a store in the middle of a cotton field invited many opportunities and dangers. I was free to explore, to learn by doing, and also to make many mistakes.

The rich alluvial plain of Mississippi County, located in the Arkansas Delta, where I lived from 1938 to 1958, produced more cotton at the time than any county in the United States. No wonder we called cotton "White Gold;" it was the lifeblood of our culture and economy. The little settlement of Mandalay (between Caraway and Manila) where our house-store stood is now virtually gone. The larger towns of Blytheville, Osceola, and Wilson along U.S. 61, which I dearly loved, have changed over the years. Still, extraordinary Arkansans continue to live and work in the county where I was born and raised.

My personal stories offer a little window into the lives of family and friends who shared similar values and traditions during what we still call the "hard years" from the 1930s to the 1950s. I hope you can imagine and gain new insight from this book into a time and place in your own life that has been long untilled.

INTRODUCTION

I DIDN'T REALIZE UNTIL YEARS LATER that my birthplace seems a bit unusual to most people. My being born in the middle of a cotton field, at a place called Mandalay, on a cold December morning always seemed natural to me. Mandalay was not in exotic Burma (now Myanmar) that we associate with romantic novels and movies. It was a tiny collection of people and buildings in the Little River Township on the western end of Mississippi County. This county occupies the northeastern corner of Arkansas, with the Missouri Bootheel to the north, Tennessee and the Mississippi River to the east, and the rest of Arkansas to the west and south. This is the "real" Mandalay to me.

Even though I truly was born smack in the middle of cotton fields, my mother, Donye Edwards Byrd, was safely ensconced in our little house, which was connected to our little store that stood at the intersection of two little roads completely surrounded by cotton fields. Doctor Harwell from Osceola, a town about twenty miles away, came to help bring me into the world. More than half of his journey was on a poorly maintained gravel road, yet he came after my daddy, George Byrd, had driven into town to fetch him. For years I heard how I came into the world screaming and how this behavior continued for years, at least according to Mother. I think she just meant I had healthy lungs and was unable to communicate in other ways, but in time I learned to talk, calmed down, and blended into my extended family.

The physical setting for most of my stories is among those fields of cotton, which we often referred to as our "fields of white gold," both because of their extravagant and glorious color but also because of their economic importance to our community and family. In our little settlement of Mandalay, not only were the fields white with cotton but as far as I know all the field hands who picked and chopped cotton were white as well. Even our clerks in the store and workers in the cotton gin were white. I had no black neighbors. Only when deliveries to our store were made from the surrounding towns did I become aware of African Americans.

Because my world was limited, isolated, and segregated at that time, it is remarkable that a woman named Ruth would become such a big part of my future. Ruth, who was black, became the most important person in my life, with the exception of my extended family. Her powerful story appears near the end of this book. My friends who already know my story about Ruth declare she was a blessing from God. I cannot disagree.

The major emotional setting for my early childhood was war. From my earliest memories, when I was about three years old in 1941 until the age of six in 1945, all of America felt the strain and fear of World War II that raged in Europe, Asia, and most of the world. I remember being so thankful for the great bodies of water that separated us from the battle fronts, hunger, and destruction. Daddy reassured me that the bad people could not reach America. This assurance did calm my little-girl fears—but only somewhat. I was fortunate that my daddy, who was born in 1901, was not inducted into the military. In 1940 men between the ages of 21 and 45 registered for the draft. This was the first peace-time draft in the history of the United States. By the end of the war in 1945, 50 million men had registered for the draft and 10 million were inducted into the military.

When we were not thinking about cotton or war, our concerns went to the threat of childhood disease. Researchers were just developing antibiotics in the mid-1930s, and it would be the mid-1940s before the public began to have access to these new medicines. Mother had barely survived typhoid fever, so our family knew from first-hand experience the dangers of "catching" something really bad. Polio was the biggest threat to us children. Because of it, my two sisters, my brother, and I endured more baths than most children in the history of the world and had to wear big, white, freshly polished shoes every day. We wanted to run barefoot like the other farm children, so we removed those clunky, fashion-challenged shoes at every opportunity, even though we lived in the middle of cotton fields and dirt was our constant companion.

Many of my stories focus on living in the rural South, but most other southern writers have never reflected "my" country experience. We didn't just live in the country; we were connected to the fields by "the store," literally and figuratively. Cotton was our major business and the store was the center of my family's life. It was also the center of commerce and the gathering place for our little community of Mandalay. On the other side of the road in front of our house-store we also ran a small movie theater that bore my name, George Ann (a unique name I grew to love), and across the intersecting road a cotton gin roared to life every fall. There were so many characters who ventured into our store that it has been difficult for me to choose only a few to highlight for these tales. And in addition to the interesting folks who lived near or patronized our store, we had lots of family members living "just down the road" who provided me with another wealth of narratives. My parents, grandparents, siblings, and I also enjoyed many unforgettably exciting trips to Memphis and to Mississippi, my parents' home state. I have tried to recapture some of these family adventures through my youthful eyes and ears. Finally, when our family moved to Blytheville, a town about twenty-four miles east and north of Mandalay, I expanded my world a little bit more and have told a few of those stories as well. All the stories in the book are true as I remember them, and the truth is that they are only a few among the many stories I could tell you.

We Southerners do love our tradition of storytelling; often our stories cause us to laugh to keep us from crying.

George Ann Byrd Danehower
Peoria, Illinois

THE STORIES

THE MUSHROOM HOUSE
AND THE COTTON FIELDS

THE MUSHROOM HOUSE

When I was a child, the house where we lived often seemed to grow overnight. I vividly remember one morning as I slept hearing a loud noise in the wall of my bedroom. Now fully awake and alarmed, I lay there peering at the wall when the working end of a big saw came through and began to create a new doorway. (No one had thought to tell *me* of this plan.) As the wood fell into my room, Daddy and another man appeared on the other side of the wall with saw in hand as if this were just a usual day at our house—and it was! So later, when I awoke to find a screened porch stretching across the back of our house, I naturally accepted it as if everyone lived in a house that grew in this odd manner. Our house grew so quickly it reminded me of a mushroom like the ones you suddenly find in your yard after a night's sleep: not there one day; there the next.

As the house grew rooms, the roofing material changed as well. I guess our house must have looked as if the architect had been

a madman. And whenever it rained, the sounds varied from room to room. It was easy to know when you were in one of the tin-roofed rooms, for example, because the sound of the rain there was ferocious. It was also a blessing that the house was never painted, for the natural color of the timber mimicked the earth from which it seemed to spring, not unlike a mushroom. This unifying element of organic color kept the house grounded and appropriate to my youthful aesthetic.

Early on, in my memory, I slept in a room close to the door that connected the house to the family store. Then I was moved to a room that seemed small and isolated from the family. Finally, I was given a bedroom that overlooked the big back porch. That room was my favorite. There was an abundance of sunlight, and I felt better connected to our family as we all navigated around one another in the house. Best of all as I lay in bed in that room, I could see the dazzling fields of cotton surrounding us as soon as I awoke.

I never felt my living situation was that different from others who lived in our little community. Yes, we did live in a house connected to a store, so we always had plenty of food and clothes at our fingertips. My mother managed the store instead of managing a house and tending to children as the other mothers did. So, on reflection yes, we did live differently from our neighbors. It was Mother's good fortune, and mine as well that her mother, my grandmother, lived just down the road from us. Mama Edwards was indisputably the best cook in the world, and she had the biggest garden I could imagine as a kid. We also had Wanda, our housekeeper, who helped to look after us and attempted to keep order in our always under-construction house. Wanda was in her mid-thirties in 1940 when she came to work for our family; leaving us only when we left Mandalay in 1944. She was a dependable and loyal woman who was kind and loving to our family. She was particularly helpful in caring for my younger brother, Donald Wayne (called Don), who had serious medical issues after measles.

The running water in the house is another memory, although not a pleasant one. It ran orange and tasted like medicine. So for drinking, cooking, and washing, we used rainwater we collected in two huge tanks located behind the house. The only tanks that I have ever seen similar to ours were rain-catchers I've seen in Australian films showing farms (stations) in the Outback. Of course, orders were firm and clear to us children: NEVER climb the ladder on the sides of the tanks and peer into the water. Of course, we kids did climb the side of the tanks and peek into them, but when we looked into the tanks we saw water so deep it frightened us. We could not swim and realized if we managed to enter the tank there was no ladder on the inside to cling to, or to climb to get us out! It wasn't something we did often, and eventually we stopped doing it altogether.

In the early 1940s, people who were looking for work and housing as they came out of the Depression often came to see my daddy. They had heard he needed workers on the farm and in the store. On one end of our house, we had rooms that our family did not live in. Again, it seemed these extra rooms just sprang up overnight as a family moved into our "spare" rooms until Daddy, Papa Edwards (who was my carpenter grandfather), and the needy family members could build a house on our "place" to accommodate them. I think Daddy and Papa built about ten to fifteen houses (really more like cabins) on our farm to accommodate new families. The "white gold" of the Delta was like the biblical manna—giving our family and the people who worked for us in the fields or the store an opportunity to improve all our lives. During this time, little brown buildings appeared all about the farm as if there were more and more mushrooms emerging from the ground.

When our new brick store was built in 1945, the old wooden store was demolished. Our old house connected to the store was then moved several yards away. I wasn't there to see this event, but I can imagine how the added-on rooms and porches separated and fell away as the original core of the house was moved. Many years later, Mother and I visited the spot where both our wooden and brick stores had stood and I asked her what had happened to our old house. She said, "Well, there it is...." She pointed to a little white-painted building that looked more like a trailer than a house. It did not resemble our old house at all. I asked her if she was certain and she insisted she was. Mother was quite elderly at this time, so I thought she must be mistaken. But the building was on the spot only a few yards from the ruins of our store. Perhaps, as I suspected then, only one or two of the original main rooms remained after the move. And, of course, the white paint had caused it to lose its mushroom-like appeal to me, and there were no great porches jutting out here and there. Gone also was the big tree with our swing hanging from its limb, and the "Australian" water tanks in our backyard were missing. I seldom return to Mandalay these days, but the next time I go there I may ask the folks who still live in what is left of our house (if there is anyone or anything there) for permission to come in. If this is truly part of my childhood home, I will be able to feel its vibe. Then again, perhaps it is best not to know for sure. It is a comforting feeling within me to believe that a bit of the Mushroom House still exists.

COTTON FIELDS

LIVING WHERE TWO COUNTRY ROADS MET and being surrounded by fields of cotton, I grew up thinking the entire world looked like mine and that everyone must be in the cotton business. Cotton was our cycle of life: spring for planting, summer for growing and chopping weeds and thinning cotton, and fall for picking and ginning. And in even later autumn, when it grows cold in Arkansas, there was sometimes cotton pulling (more like gleaning) of the last bit of the precious "white gold."

The cotton fields offered children an abundance of activity—from work to play. Some of us actually worked in the fields, but the rest of us only *pretended* to work in the fields. My favorite job, for example, was to carry the water bucket around to the workers, who were always most appreciative. They all drank out of the same dipper but usually the first dip of water was swirled around in the dipper's cup and tossed out (thereby cleaning the cup), or they just threw the cool water over their sweaty hair and hot faces. Then dipping again, they took in great gulps as the water entered their mouths.

But being the water girl had its danger too, as I learned one particular day. I was traumatized when a pack of wild dogs began to chase me as I left the weighing wagon with a full bucket of water. The dogs, sensing my fear, began to snarl and bare their teeth. I began to run with water splashing all over the ground and me. I cut across the cotton rows in hope of losing the dogs, and as I ran the sharp dry hulls of the cotton bolls cut into my face and arms like needles. As I continued on in this panic, the dogs got to my legs and began to nip at me. Then, as if God had sent him, Daddy grabbed me and lifted me high into his arms away from the animals and held me close. The cotton pickers all came running and chased the dogs away. I was shaking so badly I could not stand. A crowd of about fifteen or twenty people gathered about to give me comfort and aid, as I lay pale and trembling on the ground between the rows. It is miraculous that I did not have an infection, at least as I recall, but I was left with a fear of dogs that is with me to this day. If I'm confronted with a dog that I don't know, I feel the same exact panic I felt that day return full force.

After that bit of drama, my water carrying days were over. But still loving the fields and wanting to help, I would join Mother at the wagon where the cotton was collected and assist her as she weighed and paid the cotton pickers or choppers for their day of work. This was hard, honest work, and the people seemed truly thankful for it. As the fear of dogs in the field grew less vivid for me, I would sometimes join the other kids in the field to pick a little cotton. I liked to feel it and put it in a tow sack that had previously held potatoes shipped to our store.

As each new cotton season began, beautiful blooms would appear, and then the hard bolls would follow. Before the bolls burst with cotton, we kids would pelt one another as if we were throwing snowballs (at this point in my life I had never seen enough snow to make a ball). Our fun never cost much because there was just too much cotton for even Daddy to miss the amount we played with. For the three months when the fields lay fallow, our house-store and the surrounding cabins looked like a group of buildings on an alien landscape.

But by late 1944, when I turned six years old, life was good, cotton was King, and there was hope that the War was drawing to a close. People were finding work, and the Depression had ended.

THE STORE:
WOOD AND BRICK

WOOD

My parents left Mississippi in the early 1930s, financing their move by selling their most prized possession, a player piano. My daddy had a contract to farm some land for a Mr. Cochran in Mississippi County, Arkansas, and this proved to be an excellent move. Daddy loved farming cotton and did it well. He also saw that supplies were needed for the growing area and that no one was providing this service. I don't know the details of building the store, but Daddy and Mother probably had Papa Edwards, my mother's father, oversee the project since he was a carpenter. Mother and Daddy lived above the store in the beginning. It was a typical wooden frame building, like something you see in Western movies. A very large, black, wood-burning stove stood in the middle of the first floor, and folks gathered around it to discuss the weather (always an important subject for farmers), their families' health, and the latest gossip. We sold a "bit of everything." Mother ran the store, while Daddy con-

centrated on growing cotton and expanding our farm.

By the time I entered this picture in 1938 my parents had built a comfortable house connected to the store. Growing up in a house attached to a store seemed perfectly natural to me; it was my "normal." The green light from a Dr. Pepper clock sign shining under the door of the store into my bedroom and the hum of the large meat refrigerator were comforting. In the warm months, only a screen door to the house separated us from the dark, quiet outdoors. I remember lying in my bed hearing a lone car in the distance on the crushed-rock road and waiting for it to draw closer. Then, the sound reversed until, like the car, it too disappeared.

Even as a child, I knew that isolation was not for me. I was happiest in the daytime, when our store was filled with people. Our original wooden store had grown so large that deliveries from wholesalers in Blytheville and other larger communities were now filling the store with products. I liked to sit on the big feed sacks that were next to the wide delivery doors and watch the men take things off the trucks.

The first black man I ever saw made one of these deliveries. I was so fascinated by him I could only stare in disbelief. Finally, I had to tell him how lucky I thought he was. He stopped and said, "Why you say that, little girl?" I said with the total innocence of a three-year-old: "Because you are already black and don't have to take a bath!" I'll never forget the roar of his laugh. He walked up to some of the customers and said, "You hear what that little girl said?" And he laughed some more. I didn't get the joke, but I remember wondering why people were laughing. You might suspect I hated to take baths, and you are right. I could think of nothing finer than having the color of skin where the black dirt on me would not show. The man was not offended and kept smiling at me as he worked.

I remember one cold late-December afternoon in 1944, just a few days after my sixth birthday, as if it were yesterday. It was to be my last birthday and Christmas in the house where I was born. My parents had plans to build a new brick store to replace our little wooden one. In addition to our store being demolished and our house moved, they felt we children needed an education that only a larger city could provide. So we left our house-connected-to-a-store and moved to Blytheville, Arkansas, with a huge population (in my childhood mind) of about thirteen thousand people. It seemed like a big city to me, but not as grand as Memphis, which I had already visited once. I didn't realize that I would never see the wooden store again; if I had, I would have lingered longer, committing to memory many details that now have faded with time.

BRICK

THE NEW BYRD'S GENERAL STORE, standing on the site where our little wooden house-store had been, was built of plain sturdy red brick with a large sign on the side of the building, heralding its name just above an advertisement for Coca-Cola. And so that no one would forget, a similar sign appeared over the front door. It was definitely not a beautiful place with fine landscaping—it was what it was meant to be: a place that provided good-quality merchandise at a fair price for the convenience of our customers.

Two large gas pumps and a big Phillips 66 sign now stood at the intersection, seemingly standing guard over our store. We sold a wide variety of goods. Almost every weekend and during the entire summer, my two sisters, my brother, and I worked at the store. We did so until our mid-teens. I pumped gas, dipped ice cream, sacked and weighed potatoes by the peck, marked prices on the canned goods, sliced cold cuts on the big electric slicer, made sandwiches for the farmers, sold stamps (since we were also the local post office), sold clothes, Red Wing shoes, Fruit of the Loom material by the yard , and whatever else people would buy. I never sold the large items such as plows and seed for the farms, but the adults did.

What I seemed to really excel at was being the butt of customers' jokes. Regular patrons knew that I would seldom ask for help from the adult workers, so I was easy prey. It took me a while to figure out that there was no such thing as a "left-handed" monkey wrench, for example. (I won't tell you how long I searched for one of those, to the great amusement of everyone in the store.) The other gag on me was the flipping of a coin. It seemed simple enough to me to win, since they told me "heads they win and tails I lose." I caught on to this trick rather quickly since everyone standing around would laugh as I "lost" either way. But truth be told, I enjoyed the fun and laughter even if it was at my expense, because it was never mean-spirited.

I remember disappointing Daddy only one time when I worked at the store. I decided to help myself to a huge ice cream cone and hide behind some boxes under a counter and read a Mary Marvel comic book. Well, I was spotted by someone, and as my daddy cleared away the boxes, he said to me very sternly, "George Ann, you come out of there and help the customers! One day you are going to appreciate the education you are getting here."

Now that the store business was doing so well, my parents hired Miss Hollis and Mr. Homer. Miss Hollis lived in Mandalay's most beautiful white-painted house, raised up high off the ground in seeming anticipation of unwanted high water. Mr. Homer's house was a tiny little place across the road that looked like one of our little mushroom cabins. The two of them became my parents' "right and left hands." Daddy began to spend less and less time managing the store, since he had my capable mother who seemed to enjoy being a businesswoman and the responsible help of Mr. Homer and Miss Hollis.

In fact, Daddy had only farmed for Mr. Cochran for about three years. Since the store business proved to be so profitable, he was able to begin to buy his own land. The Cochran family became lifelong friends, and my daddy always appreciated the "hand up" that Mr. Cochran had given when he and Mother had first come up from Mississippi to Arkansas. When Daddy did appear in the store, it was usually to discuss business with the local farmers. He had a little office space in the back of the store that was centered around his big safe. As time went by, he became a kind of informal local banker, helping many people with their financial needs. I can still see Daddy at the back of the store in his khaki pants and short-sleeve light blue shirt, with his hat pushed back off of his forehead and standing by the safe that was almost big enough to step into. He and one of the farmers would be in conversation about a loan to carry the man through the winter if his crops had been bad that year.

As the store business expanded, my parents purchased vacant lots in the nearby towns of Caraway, Manila, and Blytheville and made plans to build new stores at these locations. We even had lumber in a huge shed close to the barn that was to be used for the new buildings. Then two things happened. First, Daddy found it difficult to turn management over to someone outside of our family to run an expanded chain of stores; and second, it turned out that cotton farming was his true vocation. My daddy's passion, energy, and priorities went into that business full speed ahead for the rest of his life. (It is ironic to me that Mr. Sam Walton, also from Arkansas, years later had the same basic concept for a chain of general stores that Daddy had many years earlier. So, while there is a Walmart, there is no Byrdmart. Too bad for my heirs!)

DRIVING, CIGARETTES, AND GUNS

It was hard not to show the joy I felt when one of my parents would ask me to drive a customer home. I don't know of anyone who wanted to drive a car more than I did as a young girl. I practiced every opportunity I had by driving up our driveway and then back, and by age eleven I felt accomplished. So, sitting on a big cushion that allowed me to see over the steering wheel, I was in the driver's seat, so to speak. I was just three years short of having a driver's license, since in Arkansas back then we could get a license at age fourteen and driving at such a young age was not unusual in farm country—but maybe it was for most girls.

When asked to drive a customer and/or their purchases home, I would just say, "Okay," as nonchalantly as possible. I thought that if I showed too much joy, my parents would take this privilege from me, believing I was up to something. I have to be honest here, however; whenever I was asked to drive "Uncle Walter" (who was not related to us in the slightest), it always put a damper on my enthusiasm. "Uncle Walter" had, in my experience, never taken a bath or shaved. And he

chewed tobacco and spit the juice out the car window. He smelled of urine and the rot from the turnip size, oozing tumor on the back of his neck. On my return to the store, even with all the windows down, "Uncle Walter's" foul odor lingered in the old family Chevrolet I drove, and it stayed in my nostrils for hours after I got back to the store.

But I was completely, absolutely, ridiculously delighted to drive all other customers. I would load up them and their supply of groceries into the Chevy, slipping a pack of cigarettes under the car seat for myself, and wind my way down the loose gravel roads, minding not to speed since I knew gravel could "throw me." The gravel sometimes turned to dirt roads, depending on where a customer lived, and then I had to navigate through deep ruts, sometimes with standing water, and often cross small, narrow, handmade bridges (many built by my daddy) over deep or wide ditches. All of this responsibility I relished. After the customer and groceries were delivered, it was time to pull out the Kools and puff as many as I could before I returned to the store. Just before getting to the store, I would throw the nearly full pack of cigarettes out of the car window. This little scenario was repeated numerous times. Some fortunate guy who found one of those almost full packs of cigarettes must have thanked the Lord for his good fortune.

Sometimes, friends from school would join me at the store. I remember Nelia, a sheltered only child, loved the freedom I had both in and outside the store. It was an unknown world to her. (In fact, Nelia was so sheltered that her mother would not allow her to use a butcher knife until she was twelve years old.) As an adult, she confided in me that she had never told her mother about the guns I owned, fearing she would not be allowed to visit me. When I was twelve, I already had a BB gun, which helped prepare me for the twenty-two, semi-automatic rifle I received on my fourteenth birthday. Now, as an adult, I can understand Nelia's mom's concern, but it was a different world back then.

Our daddy took my younger brother, Don, and me on little hunting trips. He taught us the safety and seriousness of guns, and I did respect and do remember this education. At summer camp on White Mountain in Hot Springs, we had riflery as one of our activities. I won several ribbons for my ability and knowledge, thanks to Daddy's training. I liked target and skeet shooting best, although I shot a few rabbits and turtles. I never did want to kill things, but part of Arkansas culture was hunting and knowing how to use a gun, and I still respect that.

Even though this story is about me as a kid, while writing about how guns were part of my life back then I have to include this anecdote from when I was just nineteen. When I married my husband, Ches, in 1958, I was unpacking my belongings, including my guns, at our first apartment. (By this time, I had acquired a WWII Beretta and a Smith and Wesson pistol.) I looked at Ches, who was also unpacking his belongings, and said, "Hon, where are your guns?" He replied, "I don't have any." The words just fell out of my mouth in disbelief: "You don't have any guns?" Ches is from Arkansas, too, and in fairness to him, he is not now and never has been a wuss! But due to the death of his uncle at age twelve in a hunting accident and because as a teenager he was seated next to a good friend who was accidentally shot in the back by their mutual friend with a supposedly "unloaded" gun, Ches had wisely chosen not to make guns one of his passions. In school, he was too busy being captain of the boxing team, a varsity football player, a first basemen and sometimes pitcher, and a champion ping-pong player. So there!

THE MEDICINE MAN, THE WITCH THE TB LADY, AND TIGHT

THE MEDICINE MAN

We may have been isolated from larger communities in Mandalay, but nonetheless we had our share of memorable characters who somehow found us. The Medicine Man, to my knowledge, was a one-time-only event involving a fast-talking huckster who promised "miracles" to all who bought his "tonic." As a young girl, I was immediately intrigued when he arrived one afternoon in his old colorful truck and began to remove a movie screen, speakers, and benches from the truck's bed. It didn't take him long to get the music going over the speakers; and it magically didn't take long for our customers from miles around to find the source of the music. Evidently my daddy had made arrangements to allow this "side show" to take place next to our store. Knowing Daddy, he probably received a rental fee for the use of the space and perhaps a percentage of the profits from the sale of the "medicine."

The Medicine Man stood in the bed of his truck so he would be elevated above the crowd that had gathered. Dressed in a shiny, well-worn black suit and dingy white shirt with a thin black tie about his neck, he was a curiosity. Even as a kid, I realized a very impressive event was going to occur. If you set up a movie screen and played music over a loudspeaker, I was drawn to it like a moth to flame. Knowing there was going to be a movie, I grabbed a good spot on a bench right in front of the screen as soon as it was set up. It never crossed my mind that it had to be dark before the movie would be visible out-of-doors and that the primary reason for this whole setup was to sell the "elixir."

I continued to sit for a couple of hours, waiting for what I thought was the purpose of this activity, the movie. Meanwhile, the crowd grew larger and larger, and when Mr. Medicine Man had all our customers gathered about the truck he began his convincing diatribe about the miracle concoction, "Hadacol." This miracle potion, I learned years later, was twelve percent alcohol and was in great demand in "dry" states or counties (those that banned alcohol from being sold). Mississippi County was a "wet," county, but Mandalay remained dry, even after Prohibition was repealed. Of course, since I was only about seven years old, I did not realize that the alcohol content was the major attraction. (In fact, I remember thinking I didn't know so many of our neighbors and customers were sick.)

I learned later that the creator of this particular mixture was not a medical person at all, but a Democratic State Senator from

Louisiana named Dudley J. LeBlanc. After years of promoting it through people like the Medicine Man, when asked why he had called it "Hadacol," Senator LeBlanc replied, "Well, I hadda call it something!"

Needless to say, customers lined up happily to part with their money. I had no interest in his "miracle," of course. I only wanted to see a movie and wished the Medicine Man would stop talking and "get the show on the road." He continued to talk and convince more and more people to try the "medicine." According to him, "Hadacol" would cure just about anything and everything, including tooth pain, earaches, stomachaches, and even nervousness. Folks around me began to sample the liquid in the bottles they had just purchased and seemed to like the taste.

It was beginning to grow dark, and eventually everyone in the crowd seemed to have their "tonic" (except me), so Mr. Medicine Man announced that it was time for the movie. Finally, I thought. (Understand, I had no idea what was about to be shown, I just loved moving pictures.) Well, if we showed B- movies at the George Ann Theater that my family ran on our property, this movie had to be a Z. The sound was so bad I could hardly understand one word. It seemed to be a movie about the mob and detectives chasing them in New York City, and it must have been one of the first talkies ever made. I didn't realize until then that there could be a movie I would not like. So I continued to sit outside in the November cold, wearing a light-weight jacket and thin-soled loafers that were not made for the frozen ground, hoping the sound and image would improve. How I hated to quit on anything, even then. (I have gotten even worse about this as I have aged.) But I was getting stiff and my feet were losing their feeling. I knew I had to give up while I was still able to walk into our warm store. I looked around as I hobbled away from the crowd and realized I was the only kid left. All the adults seemed warm, however, with some wrapped in blankets and happy as they held on to their bottles and one another.

THE WITCH

I HAVE HAD ONLY ONE ENCOUNTER WITH A WITCH during my lifetime and it came in 1944, when I was only five years old. This event was very specific. The witch was an old woman who truly fit the stereotype. She had only visited our store a few times, but the word was out that she could remove warts. It happened that my mother and I had become disgusted with the host of warts that had taken up residence on my knee. There was a huge one and many small "babies" (as I called them). When this hunched over, wrinkled witch, wearing multi-layers of clothes, came into our store one day, my mother grabbed me and sat me on the store counter. The witch looked at the mess on my knee. She then took her bony-clawed hand, reached into her pocket, and retrieved nasty looking paper that she immediately rubbed over the warted knee. My mother supplied the requested match and then the witch burned the paper she had rubbed over my knee. I was then given very simple but quite specific instructions to do an easy task at the break of sunrise the next morning.

Afraid of missing the sunrise, I forced myself to stay awake all night so I could complete the witch's directions. To ensure that I could stay awake, I asked to spend the night at my grandparents' house near ours, since Papa and Mama Edwards were very loud snorers. Just as the sun rose, I was to take a clean dishcloth and hide it outside under the steps that led into the house. That was it!

The hard part was staying awake, even with the snoring, but the roosters helped me with their crowing at sunrise. It was a bonus I had not expected. I took the witch's directions very seriously and did as I was instructed with the dishcloth, and that was the anticlimactic end of the adventure. For the first few days after the experience, I looked at my knee off and on throughout the day. The wart "family" was still there. After a week or so, I forgot to keep looking and one day, to my utter surprise, I noticed that all the warts were gone. As to the witch, I never saw her again.

THE TB LADY

As I remember some of the characters who came to our store, I will never forget the TB Lady. We called her the TB Lady because everyone knew she carried the dreaded disease with her and really was to be pitied. Tuberculosis was such a horrifying and serious disease in the 1940s that if you even heard the letters, "TB," you felt sick to your stomach. Don't ask me why the TB Lady was out and about or why she came into our store. I suppose she had no family members who could shop for her and she needed supplies. When she would enter, Daddy would grab us children and herd us into the house on strict orders not to enter the store until he gave the all clear. He must have feared we might fall ill with the dread disease if we even breathed the same air she had breathed. The TB Lady's illness scared the bejeebies out of me. I wondered if she had touched anything in the store that might make my parents or Mr. Homer or Miss Hollis, who worked for us, contract the disease.

It was like Moses parting the water. People moved away from her as fast as they could and gave her lots of space. When I peeked out of our house door, I would see my daddy in the store helping her with her supplies. He stood back a bit, but not as far as the others. Of course, after we got the all clear, I was still concerned about lingering TB germs. This was before antibiotics. It's amazing how any of us survived all the diseases that surrounded us.

TIGHT

Tight was an interesting character. It took me a few years to catch on to his nickname. He was everyone's friend yet a "ne'er-do-well" kind of guy. He would come to the store and loaf around and make eyes at the ladies. No one seemed interested, since they knew "Tight was tight," as they used to say, from too much alcohol.

For some reason, probably because he could be hired on the cheap, Daddy used to employ Tight to make "dirt-runs" over to our property nestled next to the Right-Hand Chute of Little River. There, by this tributary, good dirt could be mined for free. It was useful for the construction that continued constantly around our new store. Not trusting Tight with a truck, however, Daddy had him drive a wagon drawn by a couple of old, safe mules.

Well, we kids could not stand not being part of such fun. We begged and pleaded with our parents to allow us to help Tight get the dirt. It was a hayride plus. Poor Tight seemed overwhelmed from the beginning. There were about seven of us kids bouncing in the wagon and ready with our buckets and shovels to pitch in. It was a fun-filled ride, with our singing and laughing and Tight probably suffering from a massive hangover. We were an unlikely group. We made it to the "Chute" and started filling the wagon with the soft dark loamy soil and silt. No rocks, bottle caps, glass, or bits of paper were present in the soil. I've never felt, nor have I seen, soil like it since. The fineness of the silt was like silk. We piled the wagon high with this precious earth, and Tight began to appreciate us as he leaned on his shovel and watched us work like an army of ants.

Going back to the store the kids sat here and there on the wagon, now filled with soil. We were up high and low, with some of us dragging our feet on the road behind the wagon. I convinced Tight that, being ten years old, I could certainly drive the mules. Tight, being tight, said, "Okay." What a thrill it was to hold the reins! Today, when I see the spot where our store once stood, with only trees standing to honor the site, I think about the virgin soil that lies beneath those trees and how it felt to hold the cool, good earth and the freedom of the reins.

CANDY, FOLLOWED BY BOOKS AND A BRIDGE

CANDY

The trip from our house-store and farm in Mandalay to Memphis was only about seventy miles, but they were a world apart. We traveled on a two-lane gravel road to the famous (to us) Highway 61, which took us into Memphis, making our trip a two-and-a-half-hour drive. Of course a quick stop at the Coffee Cup in West Memphis, Arkansas, for a little breakfast was part of the routine for my daddy's trips to "the big city."

When I was four years old in 1943, I had never been to Memphis but was going to go with my daddy to buy candy for our store. I should tell you right now nothing—I mean *nothing*—pleased me more as a kid than eating candy. During the Second World War, sugar was rationed, so it seemed like magic to me that we could purchase a whole carload of candy.

Driving into Memphis, I was awed by the bluff that rose up to hold the tall buildings and sloped down to meet Riverside Drive and the Mississippi River. That is why Memphis is called "The Bluff City," among other titles. Because there had been a light snow in Memphis the day of my first visit, children were riding cardboard boxes down the snowy, mostly grassy bluff right down to Riverside Drive. Coming from the flat Arkansas Delta, sledding was something I had never experienced. I had heard of it, and here it was. If I had known then about the Wizard of Oz movie, which had come out in 1939 but hadn't yet reached Mandalay, I would have sworn I had entered Oz itself.

Our car climbed the bluff and almost immediately we were at the warehouse where men began to load our car. They filled the trunk, the seats, and the floor with boxes of candy, and my little heart was jumping with joy. I could hardly believe my ears when Daddy said I could lie on top of the boxes and eat all I wanted on our way home. I was sprawled flat between boxes and the roof of the car, but I never complained one bit.

BOOKS AND A BRIDGE

MY OTHER MEMORABLE CHILDHOOD TRIP TO MEMPHIS was again with my daddy when he took me to buy books (at the suggestion of Miss Rowley, my fourth-grade teacher). We parked the car next to the lovely tree-covered Court Square in downtown Memphis and entered the bookstore. (It was my first experience in a store that sold only one thing!) The books were displayed on beautiful wooden shelves built on gleamingly waxed wooden floors. The shopkeeper was patient and helpful, making suggestions for books that have played a crucial role in my love of books. The books encouraged my lifelong belief that women can do anything we choose to do: biographies of Clara Barton, Florence Nightingale, Marie Curie, Helen Keller, and Jane Addams were among the dozen inspiring books Daddy bought for me that day.

As we headed home, we approached the bridge that crossed the Mississippi River and connected Memphis to Arkansas. There we joined a long line of stopped cars waiting to drive over the bridge. We instinctively knew that someone had a flat tire. Flat tires were a common occurrence in the 1940s because of poor quality and/or perhaps because people were too poor to buy new ones. This bridge, named the "Harahan," had been built in 1916 and was quite a design. It is what was called a "cantilevered bridge with a through truss." This meant that a train ran down the center of the bridge and a narrow single lane for cars going west was hanging (or cantilevered) off of one side and another narrow single lane for cars going east was hanging (or cantilevered) off the other side. Hence traffic jams occurred every time someone had a flat tire. A new Memphis-Arkansas Bridge that opened in 1949 finally ended this madness, but back then all of us who were in the unfortunate western lane waited patiently until the tire was changed. What else could we do? But it didn't matter to me on that day. I had already delved into a book. I don't recall being annoyed by the inconvenience; in fact, I enjoyed the stillness of the moment.

Over forty years later, when I was serving as a panelist reviewing grants for the Illinois Arts Council, I was asked to observe a group of musicians who were performing at Hull House in Chicago. Hearing the words "Hull House" struck me like a bolt. I didn't realize that it still existed, and I had never been there except in my nine-year-old mind. I only knew about it from my reading about Jane Addams so many years before as I sat in the car waiting for the traffic to move on the Harahan Bridge. I drove from my home in Peoria to Chicago and parked my car in a quiet neighborhood on the Near West Side of the city. Then I encountered Hull House. As I walked up the sidewalk with my heart pounding, the lights were shining clearly and beautifully from the many rooms of the old house, sweet music was drifting from the windows, and an open door invited me in. As I entered, I cried with tender memories of my long-ago youth and my trip to Memphis with my daddy to buy the first books that shaped my life.

CHUCK WAGON AND AN ANGEL

I THINK WE HAVE ALL SAID: "This story has to be true; no one could make up something this fantastic." Here's one of mine. I never even told my parents (now deceased) how close I once came to catching myself on fire when I was a young girl. And only after I was married did I tell my husband about this event. Every time I see a badly burned child or hear someone say they believe—or don't believe—in angels, I relive this memory. And now I am going to tell the story to you.

I can attest to the fact that children are influenced by what they see in movies, on television, and online. When I was seven or eight, I tried to put into practice a scene I saw many times in B-grade Western movies we showed at the George Ann Theater. Remember the guy, usually named "Cookie," who was the cook for the cowboys? He was in every movie with his chuck wagon, roasting a rabbit or some other meat on an open fire, constantly turning it on a spit. Usually the pleasant scene had the men singing or joking with one another (although many years later Mel Brooks, in his movie *Blazing Saddles*, presented a very different and hilarious version of this scene that focused on beans and their aftermath).

Late one afternoon, in about 1946, I found a dead bird and wondered if I could recreate the chuck wagon roasting scene by making my own little spit over a fire and turning the bird like Cookie did in the movies. I did not plan to eat the bird; I just wanted to experience the scene. I found some wire and shaped it and strung the dead bird on it. Then with little tree branches I made holders for the spit. Next I found materials of twigs and paper I could use, to build a fire. In our store we sold coal oil, so I ran in and filled a glass Coke bottle with oil. Returning to my little cinematic scene, I struck a match to the paper and it began to burn. Then I began to pour the oil on the fire and a trail of fire immediately raced back toward the bottle. I jerked the bottle away from the fire and stared at it in amazement.

I'm not sure what I would have done next, but a man in a long gray coat, who matched the gray of the evening dusk, was suddenly standing right behind me. He seemed to appear from nowhere. He was just there. He said very firmly, "Little girl, that is very dangerous. Get that bottle away from the fire right now!" I turned to get a better look at him. I thought he must be one of our customers or a salesman, but I realized he was totally unknown to me. He was an attractive man with dark blond hair, who seemed neither old nor young. He did not look like the farmers, who had sun damaged rough skin, nor was he dressed like any salesman I ever encountered.

As an adult, I have often reflected on the man's clothing, and

I guess the best way to describe what he was wearing was a tailored, smart, and splendid light-weight overcoat. I remember that I immediately stomped out the little fire, threw dirt on it, and ran back into our store with the Coke bottle still in hand and my heart beating faster than usual. Just before I entered the store, I turned to look at the man one more time, but he had disappeared. The contrast of the light, warmth, and busyness of the store was in stark contrast to the dark and dangerous outside. It is still a jarring memory for me today. I returned the coal oil to its original container. At that moment, I still hadn't realized how close I had come to the bottle exploding and my being killed or badly burned and scarred for the rest of my life. During the years that I worked at the store, I looked for the man again and again. I thought he might return and I could thank him, but he never did.

I have wondered over the years why I never talked about this event. I believe it is because it makes me shudder, even now, to think how close I came to causing my own death in horrific circumstances. I just tried to put it out of my mind—until now. Do I really think the "man" who caused me to stop my dangerous movie reenactment was there by coincidence or luck? I absolutely do not. Believe what you will, but I believe he was an angel sent by God to protect me, so that I could accomplish the things I am meant to accomplish in my life, including writing this book.

THE GEORGE ANN THEATER

I ALWAYS KNEW IT WAS SATURDAY NIGHT IN MANDALAY when I heard Roy Acuff's voice being blasted over the loudspeaker or Ernest Tubb singing my favorite—but a bit disturbing—song, "I'm Walking the Floor Over You." (As a kid I took this song literally for years, thinking there was a person lying under our floor for some strange reason.) Anyway, Saturday night was the best time of the week during cotton chopping and picking time (late spring through fall), because the George Ann Theater, named after me (obviously), was the only source of entertainment in a radius of about ten miles from our house-store. Actually, I was never sure why my name was chosen for the movie theater and not that of either of my sisters, but I reasoned then that it was because our daddy's name was George and he had somehow just added my middle name to it. So, let's go with that.

The music began playing from the theater about two hours prior to each show. In my mind, I can still see all the people coming down the road as if being drawn by a magnet, like the cars in the movie *Field of Dreams* decades later. Most of the people in the area were still climbing out of the Depression, so they had little money to spend on frills. Almost no one owned a car. They walked, came by horse and wagon, or if lucky in a neighbor's truck. They would pile as many folks in it as possible, to come see the "picture show."

I can still see my sister, Bobbie Jean, who was almost four years older than I, working the popcorn machine, carefully handling the hot grease involved. Today it would be considered child labor abuse, I'm sure, but Bob (as everyone called her) was very cautious and mature for a nine-year-old. Our mother had taught her well. I did complain that I wasn't allowed to pop the corn, but I did the next best thing: I sold the candy, gum, and cold drinks. I was about five years old when I learned to do simple math behind the concession stand. It wasn't too hard, since everything sold for a nickel and most people had the correct change. (I am still convinced that if you want a child to understand math, teach him or her early how to buy, sell, and make change. There was a real incentive for me to learn as I saw my pile of money grow from sales.)

Some folks brought their own snacks and drinks in Mason jars, and that was fine with us (unlike in today's movie theaters). Babies nursed on their mothers, and I found this rather shocking since my mother would never have done that in a public place! The George Ann was not a fancy building, far from it. My grandfather, Papa Edwards, who was a fine carpenter, built and designed the theater. Adults sat in wooden, unpadded theater seats purchased from a company, and children sat on wooden benches made by my grandfather, in the front rows. There was heat for the chilly nights in fall, but no air-conditioning for hot summer nights. The theater probably seated about a hundred people. Movies were B-grade and in black and white, featuring mostly Westerns with a few Tarzans and—the ones I truly hated—mummies or dead people walking.

The crowd was like one big happy family. We were all neighbors and hard-working people. My daddy saw a need for some entertainment in our isolated area, so he provided it. People had worked hard for the little money they had, but with inexpensive movie tickets and snacks they felt they could reward themselves and have some enjoyment. There was never any doubt that the George Ann Theater was appreciated in our little community of Mandalay. Each movie night, after experiencing the social atmosphere and hoopla, working the concessions, and watching the movie, I always felt a little sad when all the activity ended. I usually climbed the steps to the projector room where Daddy and the projectionist, Mr. Ledbetter, who brought and ran the movie, divided the money they made that evening. It was a simple routine, repeated week after week, year after year. I am proud that our family helped make it happen.

THIEF AND MURDERER

As I've described our little community of Mandalay in northeastern Arkansas, it was filled with sweet, loving, hard-working people. That was true for everyone but one. His name was Caleb, and he lived down the road about two to three miles from our house-store. His mother often sewed for us, and his father, like most people in the area, farmed. But Caleb was born mean. Even at the tender age of five, I realized that and kept my distance from him. We all heard tales of how he was not an obedient son and not to be trusted. The gossip proved accurate when we returned home one night from the picture show at the George Ann Theater across the road.

We were watching one of the usual Western movies while, unknown to us, Caleb was ransacking our house. I'm sure now that his intent was to rob the store, but he was thwarted by heavily locked doors. However, our house was easy pickings. This night, for some reason, my mother left the show early to go home, and Caleb was still in the house, although Mother did not know it at the time. When she walked into the house, she noticed the disarray and immediately ran out of the front door she had just entered. This action may have saved her life, as Caleb thought she was chasing him as he exited through another door.

As he stepped into the night, he stopped, turned, and stood outside the door he just exited. (One of our neighbors saw this part.) Caleb stopped and raised some kind of club, ready to strike my mother if she followed him out. The rest of the family and some friends arrived just as this drama was unfolding. Caleb saw us and we saw him. He ran like a scared rabbit, or maybe I should say slithered away like the snake he was. He did take my piggy bank among a few other things.

This was just the beginning of Caleb's dreadful, sinful life. The military must have been scraping the barrel in the late 1940s when they accepted him. The U.S. had demobilized much of its armed forces in 1945 and found itself with a shortage of manpower in 1947. I don't think our family ever pressed charges against Caleb, since we felt compassion for his family. His sorry history may have been unknown to the military, or maybe they thought they could straighten him out, but it is unfortunate that he was not stopped earlier in his criminal life. It was a few years later that one of those "true crime" magazines or some such publication popular in the late 1940s and early 1950s published a story about a soldier who murdered his sergeant and the sergeant's wife. Caleb was identified, caught, and convicted of the murder. It was a most gruesome tale and included pictures. There is no need to have the details recounted, but I'll just tell you the bodies were found in a large trunk.

I wish that I had never seen the pictures or read the article. The crime is vivid in my mind to this day. Caleb went to prison, and I never followed his story after that. I did continue to see his mother, since she was a remarkable seamstress. In fact, right after the foiled robbery I was at her house and found myself looking about to see if I could find my piggy bank. That's how I knew how bad he really was. Who else would steal a kid's piggy bank?

THE COTTON GIN, HIDE AND SEEK, AND SPONTANEOUS COMBUSTION

EACH FALL, USUALLY ABOUT MID-SEPTEMBER (depending on the weather during the growing season), the cotton bolls would burst open and cotton picking would begin. White fluff began to gather on both sides of the road on our farm, particularly around the cotton gin. Mother always said every year, "My stars, it looks like snow." And it did. It was ginning season.

Ginning season began as the farmers arrived with their wagons filled with the just-picked cotton. Cotton was cradled in various wooden wagons and drawn by tractors or mules as they made their way to the gin. The sight was so ordinary to me that I never thought of its uniqueness. This season of ginning, with cotton fibers filling the air, would last late into fall, until the fields of white gold had been picked over at least twice. My world was cotton. After the cotton was ginned (meaning the cotton was dried, cleaned, and debris and seeds removed), the lint (the good stuff) was compressed into five-hundred-pound bales. These bales were then stacked and scattered on the grounds around the gin, thus creating a giant maze perfect for playing games.

From age four to about ten or eleven, we played at the gin, season after season. Naturally climbing up on the bales, sneaking around the corners, squeezing our bodies into the small spaces between bales, and flattening ourselves against the hard, compressed cotton, made hide and seek the best game of all. It never mattered that we children were repeatedly told never to play around the gin. Fun and danger lurked everywhere, which is a kid's primary criterion for fun. Sometimes while hiding among the bales, we watched the wagons of just-picked cotton pull up to the gin. A man would take a huge silver tube, that seemed as large as his body, and place it in the wagon of raw seed cotton. Out of sight to us, a switch was flipped and a ferocious noise of air sucking the cotton would begin. The man controlling the giant vacuum never stood inside the wagon and seemed to respect the strong force of air as he manipulated the enormous tube. The cotton would disappear from the wagon and enter the gin.

Through the wide-open side of the gin we could see the cotton as it reappeared as a fast-moving white waterfall. Where it fell, I do not know. To be honest though, we children never went inside the cotton gin. Its deafening motor's CHUG, CHUG, CHUG could be felt throughout our bodies when it began to gin the cotton, and often it ran well into the night. We were simply afraid to enter this strange building of metal and noise.

On the other hand, for a short time we did climb the wonderous mountain of hulls, immature seeds, and debris that was spat out of the gin. We would race to where the mountain had formed, climb to the top, and then roll to the bottom. Every day the mountain would grow, and so did our determination to conquer it. As we climbed, the mountain would give way, making our climb both more difficult and more fun at the same time. Our roll down grew faster and harder as the mountain grew higher and higher, and we were tossed in the air as we hit the bottom of the pile, which was our favorite part of the ride. No man-made slide I was ever on in my life was that much fun.

But one day something happened on the mountain that I will never forget. You might be wondering where the adults were while we enjoyed this particular forbidden game. Well, they were all working. Yes, one of them would appear once in a while and yell at us to get off the mountain. But as soon as that person left, we resumed climbing and sliding until, one day, my daddy appeared at the gin and sat all of us down at the base of the mountain and explained to us the concept of "spontaneous combustion." I had never heard these two big words before, and I asked Daddy to spell it for me and say it again. We children found it hard to believe that fire could just start on its own in the middle of our mountain and then cave in— with us still on it. This was one of the most serious discussions I ever remember with my daddy. He did not yell or threaten us, nor were we punished. After he left our mountain, we all were glum and long-faced. It was hard to believe that this marvelous playground could kill us.

We were, of course, absolutely and in no uncertain terms forbidden to ever climb the mountain again, but I secretly and on my own did it one more time. The day that I did this last climb the weather had turned cold and cloudy; I felt terrible. The fun was completely gone. With each step, I thought it might be my last. Besides, I was directly disobeying my daddy, which I (almost) never did.

It was probably no more than a week later that my friends and I went over to the gin to play hide-and-seek, and then we saw it: Our mountain had caught fire during the night and only about one-third of it was left standing. All that was left were hot glowing red hulls and smoke spewing from within the small mound that remained of our once great mountain. It is an image I have never forgotten.

HOLY ROLLERS, FOLLOWED BY SOFT CREAM AND A PICTURE SHOW

HOLY ROLLERS

Due to an illness that was believed to be rheumatic fever, I was unable to continue 1st grade, which I had started that fall of 1944 at Milligan Ridge School. Since we were still living at Mandalay, I spent a lot of time during my convalescence with my grandparents, Papa and Mama Edwards. Even after my family moved to Blytheville, I continued to rest often at my grandparents' house, which was near our store. As a six-year-old, I was treated to some unique experiences while in their care. One of those was a "holy roller" revival. I was taken only once but, as they say, "Once was enough!"

My grandparents and I took off one evening down the gravel road to what they told me was a "tent service." Bouncing along in their truck, I could see the big revival tent with its yellow light glowing through the fabric for miles before we arrived. People were milling about, and music was being played by a little band. It was like a county fair, I thought at first, and Mama Edwards was in her element. She seemed to know everyone, and they knew her. She laughed and talked as Papa quietly found us seats on three wooden folding chairs just off the sawdust aisle and close to the front of the tent. Then people found their seats and the revival began.

A man dressed in his "Sunday best" stood in front of all of us and welcomed us to the event. The music had stopped, and we were all attentive. It didn't take long for the preacher to get to the scary part of his message. He began to yell about how we were all going to hell. The more he yelled, the more people began to shout "Amen" and other things to encourage him. As the evening wore on, people became even more excited, hollering and whooping it up. Even "foreign languages" were spoken: Or at least I knew English wasn't being spoken. Then to my horror, some people began to run down the sawdust-laden aisle and roll about in the front of us. I sat there with my mouth open and my eyes taking it all in.

I looked at my grandparents and began to pray—yes, pray— that they would not go crazy and start "holy rolling" about. To my relief, they did not. When the service came to a close, the quiet was a blessing. Mama Edwards saw my distress and whispered to me that these people just got the "Holy Spirit" and that is how they expressed it.

Thankfully, I was being raised as a traditionally reserved Methodist by my parents. All they did to me at our church was sprinkle me with a carnation that had been dipped in water. The Holy Spirit apparently didn't make our brand of Methodists act crazy!

My story doesn't quite end until I tell you how this memory was triggered by a chance hearing of a song, "Down the Sawdust Trail" by Jimmy Swaggart. The words of the song begin with a childhood memory of a "camp meeting" (in my case the "revival" in a tent). The title of the song, of course, refers to the sawdust aisles I recalled from my experience that one evening with my grandparents. As unsettling as the holy roller episode was for me as a child, as an adult I am thankful for having seen it.

SOFT CREAM AND A PICTURE SHOW

OVER THE YEARS, DRIVING A GRANDMOTHER who did not drive worked to my great advantage. Mama Edwards and I had a special bond: She loved to go places, and I loved to drive her. And since she did not drive, she was never even a "back seat driver." Not once did she push on the floorboard to brake or tell me to watch out for this or that. She was the perfect passenger. I was often sent to her house when I was about twelve or thirteen years old with a delivery from our store. After she put all the groceries away, she would say, "Sister" (a pet name she often used for me), "let's go get some of that soft cream." Soft cream is what she called ice cream that was sold at the Dairy Cream in Caraway about ten miles from her house.

This trip took us down a gravel road past Milligan Ridge and then over a long wooden bridge, with no observable safety features, that crossed Ditch number 4. Deep down I did dread this part of the trip, yet I never expressed any fear to Mama Edwards. When I drove up onto the bridge, I had no side rails to guide me visually. There were no painted lines to designate my lane. Instead there were planks going in the same direction I was to be driving across the bridge. These planks were just wide enough for a car's tires. The same configuration was built for cars going in the opposite direction that I might meet (and was praying that I didn't). The two lanes were side by side, with no barrier between them. There was, as they say, "no room for error."

To get up on the bridge, the driver had to negotiate a steep climb up a man-made levee. The bridge was built so that just as you drove onto the bridge you had to turn your steering wheel a hard left on a blind curve and hope your tires would land in the right spot on the bridge. Remember, no sides on the bridge to tell you where you were!

I had to make sure my tires would hit my lane perfectly. If my turn onto the bridge was not sharp enough to the left, my front right tire might go off of the bridge. Plus, I had to be on the lookout for any other car already going one direction or the other on the bridge. Even I had enough sense to recognize the danger, so I always made this maneuver very slowly. After a safe landing on the bridge, I felt as if I had just brought in a big plane for landing. But not once did Mama Edwards flinch or show fear. Nor did I. We then drove into town and would enjoy our "soft cream" together sitting in the car. Then she would often say, "Let's go to the picture show." And of course we did.

Caraway's movie theater was a lot nicer than the George Ann Theater in Mandalay, and their movies were probably B-plus quality, instead of the B-grade films we showed. When I went to the picture show there with Mama Edwards, I quickly learned that movies could be a spectator sport. I loved the drama my grandmother brought to the movies. If a scene was exciting, for example, she would grab my arm and squeeze it and shake me a bit. If the scene was sad, she was right there with the actors, sharing her feelings with sobs and tears.

But the big event for Mama Edwards was figuring out the plot before the actors—or the audience—did. I am not exaggerating here. She would turn to me, and in a loud voice tell me (and the others sitting around us) who was doing what to whom and why. She was quite proud of her cleverness in solving the mystery of "who done it," or who was going to win the battle, or maybe who would fall in love with whom. The actors and the audience may have been clueless, but not my Mama Edwards.

My grandmother was extroverted, gregarious, sociable, and loving—thus making her the perfect grandmother for me. As I sat next to her, I remember waiting just to see what her next move might be. My mother, who was more introverted, reserved, and quiet, found that attending a picture show with Mama Edwards was akin to torture. Perhaps because I was a kid, I loved it.

INTO THE RIVER AND BUG FUNERALS

INTO THE RIVER

After the "holy roller revival" episode, my cousin Mary Esther and I talked about what I had witnessed. I tried not to embellish what I had observed at the tent show, since it really needed none. You can imagine my concern when Mary Esther invited me to watch her being baptized. I had never seen a real-life Baptist baptism in a river, which involved being dunked under water just as John the Baptist had baptized Jesus. I knew that people of certain faiths believed that to be properly baptized one's whole body, and this included one's head, had to be completely submerged under water. I had seen pictures in my own children's bible of this scary event. But being Methodist (thank you Mother and Daddy), I didn't have to do this. A little sprinkling on my head from a carnation that had been dipped in water was my baptism. I tried to convince Mary Esther that she didn't have to go through with baptism by emersion, but her parents and minister had more sway than I did. Once again, I found myself about to observe a religious experience that was way out of my comfort zone.

A large group of family and friends of those who were to be baptized met at the church to go together to the baptismal site. I ended up sitting in the bed of a truck, riding with complete strangers from her church. It was a hot day with dust blowing high behind the truck and the sun burning into my skin. I don't remember choosing to go in the truck, but I probably did since I loved the freedom and the strong breeze through my hair I felt in an open truck. I had absolutely no idea where we were going, nor did I know a soul around me whom I felt I could comfortably ask about the plan. So, on we travelled west down the gravel roads until we came to a river. Upon reaching our destination, as I recall I was told the name of the river was the St. Francis. It was a wide river, but nowhere nearly as wide as the Mississippi. It didn't seem particularly religious, or even that special of a place, since people were backing their boats down an ugly ramp to the river's edge. It definitely did not look like the picture in my bible.

We all spilled out of the truck, and I looked about for a familiar face. Then I saw Mary Esther. She and about seven other people dressed in long white robes came walking out of the nearby woods being led by their minister. This scene did look the way I pictured it would be. It was not at all like the out-of-control holy rollers. The minister walked into the water, and one by one those being baptized followed to where he was. One by one, after saying a few words, he covered their faces with one big hand, squeezed their noses shut, and put his other big hand on their backs. Then he bent them completely back into the water.

This was the only baptism I ever saw outdoors, in a river, as it must have happened to Jesus. It is a memory that has always been with me, much like my memory of the revival tent. But for this one I was glad I was there that day. Years later, when I saw the movie, *Oh Brother, Where Art Thou?* starring George Clooney, the scene and the song, "Going Down to the River to Pray," was actually quite close to Mary Esther's baptism that I had seen in the river that day.

BUG FUNERALS

I SUPPOSE MY COUSIN MARY ESTHER AND I were influenced by all the religious experiences that surrounded us: the holy rollers revival, her baptism, and of course just attending our regular church services that centered on good and evil as well as heaven and hell. These events had to have set our young minds to thinking about life and death. I can think of no other reason for us to have developed an elaborate system of funerals for bugs. Although it may seem morbid in the telling, it made perfect sense to us at the time. Also, in creating a "cemetery" for our bug funerals, we found yet another way to get into trouble that you might find interesting.

We were about nine years old when the idea of bug funerals came to us. We didn't realize then that we were brain storming, but when Mary Esther and I got together, there was always an (often crazy) idea that bloomed between the two of us. Before television, video games, the Internet, and iPhones, children often created their own activities and games. I'm not saying bug funerals were fun, but creating the whole scenario was. We spent hours and hours planning and creating the funeral services and preparing the graves for burial. Now, it is important to note that at this time in our lives neither of us had even attended a funeral, so we just sort of made up the rituals and possibilities as we went along.

Living in the country, we never had to go far to find a bug—dead or alive. We could pick up the end of any old log and bugs were everywhere. And if we didn't find a dead bug, we immediately created one! When Mary Esther and I were together, it was usually at our grandparents' house, since so many family events took place at that wonderful little house our "Papa" (who for some reason was called "Noie" by Mama Edwards) had built with his own hands. It was also more fun to have the bug funerals at Mama and Papa's house because they had beautiful flowers and some that seemed exotic. Our favorite was the spider lily. Later in life, I learned that this flower is found in many southern cemeteries—go figure. Mary Esther and I just thought the name of this odd-looking flower was perfect for our mission. There were also several varieties of sweet-scented roses and many colorful zinnias to complete the floral needs.

The two of us built roads through the "bug cemetery" that meandered around Mama and Papa's garden, and we made headstones out of special rocks we carefully selected according to their shape and color to serve our purpose. This activity always took a long time. We cleaned the rocks until they were shiny and looked beautiful. We dug little lines of graves in one part of the garden, and in another area we scattered the graves about. Each bug was carefully placed in its own little hole for his or her final rest, and we said a few appropriate words like, "You were a good bug, Amen." Little mounds of dirt were piled on each tiny grave after we placed a bug in the hole, mimicking the graves we saw in all those old B-Western movies at the George Ann Theater. (Remember Mary Esther and I were about creating our own authenticity!) Flowers or maybe just the petals were placed on top of the piled mounded dirt.

Some areas of our cemetery had tiny knolls and valleys where we dug the graves. Of course, we had built these to make our cemetery more complex, but this is where we got into trouble with our grandparents. As we dug one valley, we struck something. We began to take our time, removing the soil carefully from what appeared to be bones! Mary Esther and I were frightened about this find, but we dug on. We screamed and hollered as a boney head of a baby prehistoric animal began to emerge. We dug on and pulled bones out until we both had our fists filled with this precious treasure. There was just one thing left to do: take the bones into the house and show them to Mama Edwards. We went straight to the kitchen where we knew we would find her. She was there preparing food for one of our many holiday dinners. She looked up from the rolls she was cutting and saw our outstretched arms holding the "prehistoric" remains in our hands. Her eyes grew wide and she suddenly looked pale and began screaming: "Oh my No-IE! They dug up the cat!"

COUSINS: TENNESSEE, ARKANSAS, MISSISSIPPI

TENNESSEE

As I was growing up, my cousins became an integral part of my life. I had cousins in Tennessee, Arkansas, and Mississippi. The Tennessee bunch, however, was pretty much crossed off our list after my mother was insulted by them. To make a long story short, our parents had sent their three daughters to visit cousins in Memphis, and Mother had outfitted each of us with a brand-new sundress for church on Sunday. When we came down to breakfast that morning, our aunt was the first to arrive in the kitchen after us. She looked at our dresses, commented on our uncovered arms, and then went into a kind of tizzy. She had us twirl about in front of her, exclaiming that this just would not do! We were not fit for church, she said. She went on and on about how could our mother have sent us with such inappropriate clothes for church. Her weird diatribe went on for several minutes. She then decided that since we did not have the proper clothes for church, we would all stay home that day. She would be too embarrassed to be seen with us.

The three of us were about five, eight, and twelve years of age when this visit took place (Bob being the eldest, Sue the youngest, and I being the middle girl). We were old enough to remember, word for word, what our aunt had said to us and, even worse, what she said about our mother. When our parents came to collect us, we could not get out of there fast enough or stop telling Daddy and Mother about the experience. Our daddy supported our mother, of course, even though our aunt was his sister. As the years passed, I've actually laughed about not being fit enough for church every time I see a sign that says, "CHURCH IS FOR SINNERS." Memphis was a great city, but not great enough to ever get me to go back to my Memphis cousins' house.

ARKANSAS

VISITING MY COUSINS WHO LIVED DOWN THE ROAD from us in a place called Blackwater, on the other hand, was always a special treat. Mary Esther, who was my age, was always a willing accomplice in any of my schemes. For example, she and I once took off all our clothes except our panties at age four and sat inside old inner tubes as we floated down water-swollen Ditch number 8. Not being able to swim was of no concern to us because, in our young minds, we had the safety of the tubes. Besides, in our part of Arkansas there were no swimming pools, so our options were limited. What else were we supposed to do to cool down? We were having a grand old time in the muddy, snake-filled, disease-infested ditch until Aunt Ethel (Mary Esther's mother and my mother's sister) drove up in her car and began to scream at us.

We were yanked out of our tubes, taken to their home, and deposited in "number 2" washtubs. Water from an outside pump was poured all over our trembling bodies. Then the scrubbing began with harsh soap and a washcloth entering every fold of our ears, eyes, and personal crevices. We screamed, but my aunt screamed back louder. She had always been kind and pleasant to me. To see her in such a state caused me to wonder: What had happened to the Aunt Ethel I loved?

As Mary Esther and I began to recover from our trauma, I suggested that we two should dig ourselves our very own swimming pool. We were surprised when Aunt Ethel thought that was a great idea, and the next morning on the back porch we found two shovels laid out for us so that we could begin our new task. As Mary Esther and I marched off to the pasture to choose a site for our pool, with shovels over our shoulders, in the ninety plus degree heat, I looked back and saw a smile on my aunt's face as she turned and whispered into my Uncle Thurman's ear.

Later that day, to recover from near heat exhaustion after digging in the pasture, Mary Esther and I took refuge in her house, which—although not air-conditioned—was certainly a lot cooler than digging a swimming pool in the blazing sun. That's when I first encountered my cousins' newest pet. I was fascinated by its uniqueness. Many people have a cat or dog, even an occasional bird; but Mary Esther and her sisters and brothers had a pet squirrel. I had only known squirrels in the wild, and I had never seen one in a cage. And I don't care to ever see one again! As I put my hand close to the cage, the squirrel lashed out at me with all its force. Badly scratched, I could only yell, "Who keeps a pet you can't pet!" From somewhere within the house in a distant room, I heard my aunt yell, "Don't pet the squirrel." Timing is everything.

Now after the ditch and squirrel events, you would think I might have sought a safer venue to hang out, but I dearly loved my Arkansas cousins and they loved me. So, in spite of the pain and injuries I had received, I was not angry. We still had plans for more fun the next day.

We all slept well that night in my cousins' big old house. It was similar to my house, but it was not attached to a store. Nor did it appear to have rooms and porches added here and there. The big difference at her house was the big breakfast and the country music. I had never had two kinds of gravy at breakfast. Milk gravy was served with potatoes and red-eye gravy was served with biscuits, and I found it all to be delicious. Aunt Ethel was my mother's older sister, but that is where all similarities ended. My aunt was a great cook, laughed a lot, and always turned on the radio in the mornings to country music. This was music that I never heard at my house. I only knew what it was because Mr. Ledbetter (our projectionist) played it from the loudspeakers prior to the movie picture shows at the George Ann Theater.

After such a filling meal, the cousins and I were ready to go. Our plan was to take a walk into territory we had never been. Joining us were my older sister, Bob, and Mary Esther's two older sisters, Noma and Mavis. So, off the five of us went. We crossed the road in front of my cousin's house and avoided Ditch number 8. We continued to walk in the heat and dry weeds. As we plodded on, we finally encountered a fence we knew we just *had* to climb.

The fence was fortified with barbed wire at its top. My cousins and sister were all tall girls, so just by pressing down on the fence in a safe place three of our group were able to step over the fence. But I stood with Noma, trying to figure out how I was going to get over the fence. Since I was the runt of the group, I was unable to step over it. The collective "group think" decided to lift me over the fence. Noma picked me up to hand me to Mavis on the other side. There was just one problem: Noma dropped me on top of the barbed wire before Mavis could grab me. There I sat, unable to free myself from the barbed wire. I had to wait for all of them to lift me up and then over. We all learned that day how loud I could scream.

I was still in pain, and we decided to follow the fence and hope to find an opening so we could return to my cousins' home. We didn't have to walk too far when we discovered a spot where the fence had been knocked completely down and we could all easily step over it. To this day I cannot look at barbed wire without recalling my great barbed-wire adventure.

As a little postscript to this story, years later as an adult I was having dinner with an artist friend who is a sculptor. In discussing the creative material she used in her work, she related a story to me about her relative who was creative, but in a practical way, and had become very famous for one of his invention. "Oh really, what did he invent?" I asked. "He invented barbed wire," she said. I stopped eating, stared at her, and thought: Should I tell her my story?

MISSISSIPPI

As DREADFUL, BORING, AND UNKIND as our Memphis cousins had been, our Mississippi cousins were loving, interesting, and talented. These were actually my second cousins. Their grandmother was my great-grandmother, but I won't go into detail on all of this. Just know that this was my mother's side of the family, the Edwards and Myricks. Most of them were blessed with beautiful, thick, wavy red hair, and they all had pretty smiling faces. They were gifted in storytelling and singing, as well as playing the fiddle and guitar. (Plus, they never seemed to care what clothes we wore to church on Sunday!)

In the 1940s and early 1950s, the drive to Mississippi from our home in Arkansas took much longer than it does today, since even the highways were only two lanes back then. After we got past Memphis, we entered a countryside colored with red dirt and a narrow highway that went up and down hills that were approximately the same height and close together. When you looked down the road, it appeared as if we were on the tracks of a roller coaster. The dramatic change in the color of the soil and the evenly spaced hills might as well have been a big billboard stating, "You have now entered Mississippi!" We were in Mississippi, my parent's home state, which they dearly loved but had left seeking a more prosperous future in Arkansas.

We would finally make it to New Albany, Mississippi, after stopping in Holly Springs to eat at a restaurant on The Square, where I always ordered the "blue plate special."(For some reason, I thought it was special because they said it was, not because it was cheap.) The food in Mississippi was always cooked to my liking, particularly the desserts. I knew too that once we arrived at my cousins' house, Aunt Lela would cook a feast for us on her wood-burning cook stove, where she was an expert.

We never went empty handed. Daddy always stopped at the store in New Albany and bought all sorts of foods to share, and Mother always took boxes and boxes of gently worn or new clothes from our store. We would arrive at their big, unpainted, wooden home located in a place called Lone Star and find the entire clan waiting for us on their wide front porch that was unscreened and stretched across the whole front of the house. We were welcomed with arms opened wide and faces smiling warmly.

Uncle Charlie, the head of the family, had been a hero in World

War I. He was gassed by the Germans and still suffered with poor lung capacity. Nevertheless, he did his best to provide for his family and the many other relatives who found their way to his door. In addition to working the small family farm, he served his community as the Justice of the Peace.

Our being at their house had the feeling of Christmas, even in the middle of the summer. After the cheerful greeting we always sat down to dinner, usually of fried chicken, fresh vegetables from their farm, and banana pudding or homemade pie or cake. All this was eaten with gusto and much conversation. When we were all totally satiated, we turned our attention to the distribution of the clothes that Mother had brought for everyone. It was like a style show with much oohing, ahhing, and laughing. The aunts and uncles and cousins all appreciated the gifts, and I learned deep down that giving is the best feeling in the world. They could not possibly have been happier than I was when I saw their joy and felt their gratitude.

After all of this celebrating, the talent show began. My younger sister, Sue, and I always came prepared. We brought our tap shoes and dance costumes and had worked up a little act. We carried a portable record player to make our performance seem (at least to us) very "professional." Someone would start the music and another person would open the screen door from the house onto the porch. Out we came with our arms bent and held up in front of our chests, our feet up on their balls (imagine putting out a cigarette) first the right foot and then the left, and once in front of everyone we performed our (infamous) jumping forward and back, clapping our hands, and then what we called the "shuffle ball change." With our shiny white satin costumes with black music notes on them, we must have been a sight, but no audience has ever been more respectful or applauded more enthusiastically.

After our stellar dance routine, it was cousins Mable and Hazel's turn to perform. Now the real talent came forth. I can still see the two of them seated in the big porch swing, picking up their guitars and singing original songs of our Irish ancestors in sweet, pure, close harmony. They took our breath away. This was before blue grass was called blue grass, as far as I know. To us it was simply "the music of the Mississippi hills." Then their brother Thomas picked up the fiddle and played it as if it were part of his body. What evenings these were! The night sky in rural Mississippi was aglow with a zillion stars, and the Milky Way was so vivid it was as if you could reach out and touch it. No one wanted these evenings to end, but exhaustion finally arrived. We all slept well, loving one another and sharing in God's blessings as only extended family can do.

As years went by, our trips to Mississippi became less frequent as we all became busy with our own families. Years passed, and then like magic we all began to write, call, and visit again. I learned that Hazel and Mable, soon after our childhood visits ended, began to sing on the radio at WELO and WNAU in the Tupelo-New Albany area. Hazel continued her music career by singing with a blue grass band, performing at many festivals throughout Tennessee,

Kentucky, and Mississippi. Mable's collections of stories about Mississippi won several awards and were collected by the University of Mississippi (Ole Miss), becoming part of its permanent collection of Mississippi literature.

My sister and I, on the other hand, hung up our tap shoes soon after our Mississippi performances. Had our family get-togethers been a talent competition back then, we all know who would have won.

THE FIRST DAY OF MY FIRST 1ST GRADE

Beginning the 1st grade is a memorable experience for many, and I got to do it twice! Here is the story of the first time.

I was five years old when I entered the 1st grade. At this time, we were still in our house-store in Mandalay. About two miles away, at a place named Milligan Ridge, was my school. The large rambling white building, with its huge windows and green shutters, looked more like a fine country estate than a traditional school. It was set back amid a large grove of trees on a big curve of a gravel road, with a store and cotton gin across the road. It looked much like our own little community of Mandalay, except it had a school. I had been in the school building only once before, with my grandmother, Mama Edwards, to attend a performance by a blue grass band. That was my first introduction to live music, and it might as well have been the Chicago Symphony so unsophisticated was my musical taste at the time. Having had that seminal experience at the school, I was prepared to go there "for real" as soon as school started.

In cotton-farm country, school often started late in the fall, since so many children worked with their parents in the fields. Finally, the big day arrived in the fall of 1944, and the night before my first day of school I was allowed to pack my own lunch. I walked into the store after all the customers were gone, and my parents said, "George Ann, just take what you want. It's your first day of school!" Don't ask me why, but they allowed me to fill a huge grocery bag with enough food to last me for about a month.

I was up early the next morning, filled with excitement to get on the bus, with only my big bag of food slowing me down. As the bus pulled up to our house-store, my older sister, Bobbie Jean, dashed out the door and I followed dragging my bag of food. Bob (as everyone called her) knew the routine since she was already in the third or fourth grade. She had gotten off to a bad start when she began school, with a bad case of separation anxiety in 1st grade. But by the time I entered school, Bob had adjusted and wanted to ensure that I didn't suffer the same way she had. She didn't have to worry: I was raring to go.

The school bus ride was my first ever, and I found it to be like a ride at the carnival. I didn't want the fun ride to end. At each house or groups of houses, the bus doors would open and more children would get on, and then the bus would take off again, bouncing along the gravel of State Road 158. I couldn't believe I would get to take this ride every morning before school.

It was a brief bus ride from Mandalay to Milligan Ridge since the bus never deviated from our main straight road. Upon our arrival we were met by a phalanx of teachers as the doors of the bus opened. It was a short walk to my classroom with our teacher and the other 1st graders. When I saw our room, I felt as if we were entering a magical space. Colorful pictures filled the walls and long, low tables and chairs fit for our little bodies were scattered about the room. Big windows, with sunlight and a warm fall breeze blowing in, held me in awe. This was all too good to be true, I thought to myself.

The teacher, Miss Jackson, immediately gave us fun activities to do with construction paper, scissors, glue, and crayons. My body felt comfortable in the "kid size" chair set around a table with about five new friends seated with me. It took me no time to get absorbed into my art project, with my head bent down cutting and gluing, when a painful blow came down on my head. To this day, I remember the deep, sharp, unexpected pain I experienced. Going from peaceful bliss to such a disorienting occurrence was a surprise of the greatest magnitude. I screeched loudly as only a five-year-old girl could screech and turned to see how and what had caused this unexpected pain. There he stood—a big boy for a 1st grader. He had his arm raised again to bring the same blow down on the girl seated next to me, but Miss Jackson was able to grab his arm in midair and stop his devilish act. It suddenly seemed to me that not all was paradise in my classroom.

His name was Jimmy, and he was immediately escorted from the room. We later learned that Jimmy was not "right." (I know

now, as an adult, that I should have pity on him, but it's still going to take me a little more time, even after all these years.) Jimmy may have been "slow," but he was a boy who had perfected the art of causing pain. After the teacher calmed me down, she told me Jimmy would be coming back into the classroom and she would watch him more closely. Well, so would I. He would not catch me, George Ann Byrd, unaware, ever again. I spent the rest of the day keeping one squinty eye on Jimmy, meeting his squinty gaze back at me. So ended the first day of my first 1st grade. I lost a little of my eagerness about school, but after a few days Jimmy did not return (I never did learn why), and I could relax once more without fear of him.

Just weeks after this inauspicious beginning of my educational career, I became ill with flu-like symptoms that resulted in my being confined to bed for many weeks. Not only was Jimmy gone from the classroom, so was I. During this convalesce I lay in my bed that overlooked the big screened porch in our house-store and watched the activity in the cotton fields. I never felt isolated since Wanda, our housekeeper, was there as well as assorted family members popping in and out of my room. Doctors from the nearby towns of Blytheville and Osceola came to administer medicine and opinions. My heart was checked over and over, because the doctors heard something irregular. To this day I don't know what the diagnosis was. Was it rheumatic fever or just the flu? No antibiotics or fancy technology was available back then, so my body just had to fight it off. I was visited by some of my parents' friends who brought gifts of candy, coloring books, and crayons. For the first time in my life, I just wasn't interested in candy, and I think that is when my parents knew I was really very sick. Mr. Nunley, one of our wholesalers from Blytheville, came with a whole box of Hershey candy bars, knowing that they were my favorite. He stood at the end of my bed with such a concerned look that I thought maybe this was my end. However, by Christmas I began to rally, and it was a good thing too, because we were moving into our new home on a paved street in Blytheville. But I had missed almost the entire first semester of 1st grade and was never to return to Milligan Ridge Elementary School.

THE BIG MOVE

THE FIRST TWO QUESTIONS I REMEMBER ASKING when I learned we were moving to Blytheville were: "Will our house be on a paved street?" and "When do I start school again?" This was undoubtedly the most eventful time of my young life, because the events included a new house, a new store, and the flowering of my relationship with my grandmother—and they all occurred around my sixth birthday. I didn't linger to say good-bye to my old house, since I was focused on what lay ahead in Blytheville. It sounds as if this move was across the United States, when in fact it was only about twenty-four miles east of Mandalay. We didn't even move out of our county of Mississippi, Arkansas. We just left the gravel road at Manila and traveled on Highway 18, which was still very narrow but completely paved, into Blytheville. We now lived only six miles from the Mississippi River.

When we arrived at our new house, I was delighted to see a straight cement walkway leading up to our front door and a huge Sycamore tree in the side yard. Our white-painted house stood on the corner of Holly and Madison Streets, with the neighbors' homes all about us, forming a real neighborhood. Sidewalks across the street invited roller skating, and our paved street meant smooth and easy bike riding. This was important to me, because I had long felt "deprived" (although I didn't know what that meant and certainly wasn't) by not being able to skate or ride my tricycle and later my bike on the country gravel and dirt roads in Mandalay. On the other hand, there would be no more listening to the lonely sounds of distant cars coming and going on the gravel roads or to the grumbling of the cotton gin late into fall nights, and our home would not be connected to our store, which was one of my favorite things in the world.

I remember what I was wearing that day as I walked up to our front door. Mother had bought matching navy wool capes for my sisters and me from the Sears and Roebuck catalog that made me feel very special. Our new house was not a mansion, but to my six-year-old eyes it might as well have been. Some of the significant memories I recall about the house were that we now had a huge kitchen, two bathrooms, and floor furnace grates we could stand on and feel warm air surrounding our bodies. My parents had all the furniture in place the day we arrived. Almost all of it was new, causing me to feel I was in someone else's house. The formal dining room was a wonder to me, with its elegant shining Duncan Phyfe style furniture and its beautiful carpet under the table. Outside, the surprises continued when I discovered a garage for our car attached to our house. And, best of all, just across our backyard behind the hedges stood a Mulberry tree and a separate small, white cottage for a maid that we were planning to hire.

Our neighbors welcomed us right away with gifts of homemade cakes and other delights. Children were everywhere. Unable to abandon the grocery house-store concept completely, my daddy had cases of some of our favorite canned foods, such as Pride of Illinois Corn and Freestone Peaches, stored on shelves in the garage. It's hard to break old habits. We did find it very convenient to have milk delivered to our front door, along with *The Commercial Appeal*. I shared a bedroom with my older sister, Bob, and I liked that. She always gave me a secure feeling.

Our store had always served as the local post office for the Mandalay area, but being in Blytheville meant we now received mail just as our neighbors did. We had a mailman with an official uniform who carried the mail in a big leather satchel on his back. He always knew that he would get ice water at our house on hot days as he made his rounds in the neighborhood. Since some folks were still without work, our house was somehow marked as a place where "hobos" could get a handout of a meal. It seemed there was a "poor soul" knocking on our back door several times a week. This new house was a happy place for me, although I did miss having a store connected to it. All I had to do in Mandalay if I wanted to socialize or get teased was walk through the doorway from our house into the store and immediately there were characters everywhere. In Blytheville, I had to work a little harder meeting such characters.

As I adjusted to our new home, our big new brick store was being built. I only recall seeing our store once as it was being constructed. Whenever Mother drove to Mandalay to oversee the building project, she took me with her and dropped me off at Mama Edwards' house (so I could continue to rest from my illness) and collected me on her return to Blytheville. However, I often chose to remain overnight at my grandparents' home. But after a few months, Mother took me to see the new store before she deposited me at Mama Edwards' house. The brick walls of the new building were already up, and I ran through its dark vastness barefoot on the ground that was soon to be covered with a cement floor. The size of it was amazing to me. Our old wooden store and house could have fit inside the new store, with ample room left for another wooden store and house to fit inside as well. It was beginning to grow warmer and the store was growing fast.

It's hard giving up old habits, so our new store also had living quarters at the back of it. My father drove back to Mandalay every day overseeing the new construction, and my mother was home with us more than I ever remembered. There was no Mama Edwards in Blytheville to do the cooking for us, so Mother cooked. I remember being surprised that she could make delicious chocolate pies and pineapple upside-down-cakes. When did she learn this? But these circumstances didn't last long.

Mother hired a woman named Jesse to oversee the house, do some cooking, and tend to us kids. Jesse had her own family, so she never lived in the little cottage set behind our hedges. She was a wonderful cook, making angel biscuits that were so light and tender they almost levitated off the plate. Jesse was kind to us kids, but her first love was cooking. Since she was always busy in the kitchen, I just went my way and she went her way, but I did show up for her meals!

I was anxious to get back into school, only to learn that my parents had met with Miss Turner, the supervisor of elementary city schools in Blytheville, and had discussed my situation. Since I had started school when I was five and had basically missed that semester of school and I still seemed to tire easily, they decided it would be best for me to wait until school started in September in Blytheville and begin 1st grade again. This was a blow for me. What would I do with all this time?

Well actually I slept a lot. I spent much of that winter and early spring in Mama and Papa Edwards' house, near Mandalay. When I was not resting, Mama Edwards gave me fun jobs and allowed me to help her. I learned to churn milk to make butter, and we often made my favorite—tea cookies and homemade ice cream. To this day, when I go into a bakery I've never been in, I always check out their sugar cookies. Over the years, I have searched for the taste I remember of those tender, pale-yellow, delicious cookies from my grandmother's kitchen, but none have come close.

Also, to pass the time, my grandmother and I listened to her favorite soap operas, *Lorenzo Jones and his wife Belle* and *Ma Perkins*, on a huge floor model radio. It seemed odd to me that I began to get interested in the fictional lives of the characters and looked forward to tuning in the next day.

I watched Mama Edwards wring the heads off of chickens, and then with a morbid curiosity I watched them hop about headless. Then she taught me how to clean them. I can still smell the hot, wet feathers as I plucked the chicken. I gathered eggs from the hen house and collected potatoes and onions that were stored in the smokehouse under a dusting of pickling lime powder. Amazingly, my grandmother never seemed to tire of my endless questions; certainly, that was the case when I watched her can the last of the winter garden. Now, that was a real production! She never needed a book to guide her through her cooking or canning. Often, and best of all, we would just sit and talk as she tatted beautiful edges on pillowcases.

Spring finally came in 1945 and, much to my surprise, jonquils popped up along the walkway to the front door of our new house in Blytheville. I was finally feeling stronger after my long illness and began attending Sunday school at the Methodist Church, where I made many new friends. As summer came, the ice cream man appeared. He was an enormous black man with only one leg. He and his ice box were pulled down our street by an old mule hitched to a wagon covered with a colorful canopy. He rang a bell and called out, announcing his presence. He soon learned that I would be one of his best customers. Of course, I had to inspect each treat, making sure his mule's hairs had not gotten on my ice cream. I also found there were some other wonderful characters in town, such as the one-armed tamale man who sold tamales from his wooden cart on Main Street. I had never heard of tamales, and I was totally fascinated with this new food and enterprising man.

But the most beautiful and impressive sight for me in my new hometown was the Greek Revival Post Office (of course then I only knew it was a big and majestic building). To complete this unique sight and setting was a man who was usually standing in front of the post office selling what appeared to be hand-made bright yellow canaries on strings attached to wooden dowels. He had hundreds of these birds for sale. When it was whirled about, the feathers would move on the air and the resulting whistling sound created a most pleasant song. To add a bit of variety to his wares, the "bird-man" sometimes sold pinwheels attached to dowels that were fun to hold up near the opened window in our car as we were driven home from downtown Blytheville; there was no air-conditioning in our cars—but you don't miss what you don't have! Life in town just got more interesting all the time. Now I only had to wait a few weeks and I would be in 1st grade again. How would it compare to the school at Milligan Ridge? I hoped no crazy-mean Jimmies would be in my class.

THE FIRST DAY OF MY SECOND 1ST GRADE

No bus with its carnival-like ride took me to school from our new home in Blytheville for the first day of my "second 1st grade." My daddy drove me early to my new school—only about three little town blocks away from our house—and parked his car on a side street next to the building. We walked up six big cement steps and I was confronted by an imposing two-story brick building, the Blytheville Central Grade School. This austere building was in stark contrast to the little white-painted wooden school I had briefly attended. But the most dramatic difference at first glance was the location of my new school. It overlooked one of the busiest highways in America, whereas my old school was nestled among trees set in the curve of a country rock road. Highway 61 was known as the "Blues Highway" (but to the locals it was Chickasawba Avenue as it snaked through our town). It connected New Orleans and Memphis to St. Louis, located to our north; all this traffic passed by my new school, day after day. I definitely was *not* in the country any longer.

With so many new things to digest, it seemed to be a thousand miles away from my secure little world. Daddy opened one of the two large wooden-and-glass doors and we stepped inside to my second beginning of my lifelong education. The smell of the building hit me first—not unpleasant, but it had a distinctive odor of cleaning oil and wax. The polished walls and floors were built of dark wood. This all looked serious to me. We walked through a big open hall, and then turned left into a smaller hall and immediately entered my classroom on the left.

The teacher, Mrs. Evelyn Willoughby, was alone in the room and rose to meet my daddy and me. She met me with a kind, sweet smile and, sensing my nervousness, began to show me about the room. I had left my previous school, at Milligan Ridge near Mandalay, midway through my first 1st grade because of illness. Now, in my new classroom I searched for something familiar, and then I spotted it. Big windows, similar to windows at my country school opened to the outside air, sunshine, and sounds. I immediately felt comfortable and connected to my new room, teeming with plants, fish, and a great color wheel. Each student had his or her own little desk with the seat molded into it. Just by lifting up the desk's writing surface, you could store your books, pencils, and paper. A huge blackboard ran the length of the room, with numbers above it and the alphabet on top of that. There was so much to see that I just stood next to my desk and spun around taking it all in. Mrs. Willoughby told my daddy he could leave, and she turned to me and asked if I would like to help her.

She showed me a simple mimeograph machine and taught me how to use it. At once I had a job and felt accepted and useful. So far so good, I thought. My teacher was young, thoughtful, and pretty, and I liked her already. The other students began to arrive, and one by one I met my new friends. I looked the group over carefully and didn't perceive one crazy-mean Jimmy (the kid who had clunked me on the head on my first day in my first 1st grade). However, I would still be on watch. We had assigned seats and sat in them as soon as the teacher asked us to. I was just beginning to get my confidence back when the teacher said for us to all stand and face the board. I understood the stand part and did so, but what did "face the board" mean? I looked across the room and realized I was the only one looking to the back of the room while all the others were looking forward, past me, at the blackboard.

Everyone else knew the code words but me. How stupid I felt! Why didn't I know this? Why did everyone get it but me? Well, the others had all learned it in kindergarten, but I had never been to kindergarten, and the phrase had never come up in my first 1st grade. I felt at that moment that I might fail 1st grade and have to start it over for a third time: my third 1st grade! But after the initial shock of realizing I had a lot to learn, I began to relax and quickly became a good listener.

Seated next to me was Gail, who helped to put me at ease. I had met her at Sunday school, and knowing her was a tremendous help getting me through the first day of my second 1st grade. How could I have foreseen that Gail Brogdon would become a lifelong friend for more than seventy years as of this writing. Oh yes, I did not have to repeat 1st grade—or any other grade—again.

THE TEST, THE WORM, AND PARALYSIS

THE TEST

Do all kids have worries even if their basic needs are met for food, water, shelter, clothing, and love? I can't speak for others, but I still managed to find a way to worry. Reflecting on what caused me the most angst during my childhood, I have settled on four major concerns: achievement tests, ringworm, polio, and—the biggest one of all, which I will tell you about in the next chapter—the Second World War.

My first worry as a child was fear of disappointing myself on the school achievement test. I remember my feelings clearly to this day. 1st graders were spared this trauma, but in the second grade the Supervisor of Elementary City Schools, Miss Winnie Virgil Turner, came to our class to explain what the achievement tests were about. Now, this was serious stuff! Miss Turner was a tall, thin, no-nonsense lady who appeared gray and starched like her clothes. I was intimidated just looking at her. Then she began to describe what we were about to encounter. Already my palms were sweating, and I had to go to the bathroom.

Miss Turner attempted to put us at ease, sensing that our little group of serious second graders was suffering some sort of group anxiety. Quickly she explained that an achievement test was something students did not pass or fail. Hearing that, I was able to take a breath; Maybe this wasn't going to be so bad, I thought. The supervisor said we would take an achievement test yearly in late spring until we finished the sixth grade. The test was to find out if we had learned what we were supposed to have learned that year. Students would find out how they ranked among their class members. Goodness, I thought, this could be embarrassing. Then the explanation got worse: The results would also tell our teachers how we ranked in the state among other students in Arkansas and then how Arkansas ranked within the whole United States. Now I was ready to throw-up! "The test would take all day," she said, and then she gave us a little example of what to expect on the test.

Her first example was vocabulary. I thought I was pretty good at definitions and spelling. We were to circle the correct definition of the word "prior." My gosh, I thought, I don't have a clue! She pronounced "prior" again and all I could think of was how do we "pry her" from the fence? (Here I was thinking back to my fence experience back in Mandalay with my cousins when they dropped me on top of the barbed wire fence!) The more I thought, the more I panicked. I couldn't answer the very first question—and it was just an example. I was trying to think how I could excuse myself with a serious, long-term medical crisis or something, but no viable thoughts came here either.

So eventually I just had to take the annual achievement test, and each year through the sixth grade in the few weeks *prior* to the testing I would begin praying that God would help me through this gut wrenching, palm sweating, traumatic experience. Not to brag, because I always believed God did it for me, I continued to rank a year ahead of my class year, year after year.

THE WORM

IF THE ACHIEVEMENT TEST CAUSED ME ANGST, the second worry of my childhood caused me more than a few sleepless nights. Saying it now sounds rather silly, but ringworm was attacking the kids in Blytheville. During the summer of 1946, when I was seven years old, there was no medication that worked very well to stop this "creeping crud." The body quite often just had to "wear-out the worm."* It would be the late 1950s before the medicine Griseoful-vin would be available to successfully treat ringworm on the scalp and, of course, we were not aware of this future medication and it didn't matter since we were living in the present. We needed help

---

* *Years later I learned that ringworm really wasn't a worm, but a fungus that gave the appearance of being a worm. Perhaps if we had known that in 1946, we would have felt a little less apprehension.*

then! All sorts of treatment were tried, but the worm just seemed to keep spreading. This was obviously a real crisis. The city was on edge, and we just didn't know who would be the "next to go." As I recall, our main picture show in Blytheville, the Ritz, was closed briefly for a thorough cleaning during the epidemic. Even my dear friend, Sally McCutchen, whose family owned the Ritz, had her personal brush with "the worm." Her little cousin from out of town came to visit for a few days. To her horror, when she opened the door to welcome him—there he stood with his shaven head that had been painted purple!

The worst part of this saga is that the worm attacked our heads. Oh, it could show up just about anywhere on the body; but having it on the scalp was life changing. At least it changed that person's life for several weeks during that summer. If I had contracted ringworm on my head, my hair would have been sheared off like a sheep sheared of its wool. Yes, this is what happened to the poor kids who got ringworm on their scalps. The loss of hair was bad enough, but now the ringworm itself was visible, with its little raised ring on the child's scalp. Now with no hair and an inflamed eruption on their children's scalp, creative mothers sought ways to cover the mess. Beanies were born. These little skull caps appeared seemingly overnight and dotted our townscape with children fixed underneath their caps with miserable looks on their faces.

When the Ritz opened again, we were all a little leery of contracting the disease, but our mothers solved this problem too. We took our own towels from home and stood in line at the picture show with our towels rolled up under our arms, so we could place it on the theaters' seats behind our heads. I remember seeing a few kids in line who had been sheared, but new hair was sprouting, so they were on the road to recovery. Some beanies had been embellished with do-dads and art to personalize them and, perhaps, to lift the spirits of the affected child. The worm epidemic lasted only that one summer, but its memory has lasted me a lifetime.

PARALYSIS

MY CHILDHOOD RINGWORM WORRY, however, paled in comparison to my fear of polio. This was because no one knew what caused the disease and there was no known prevention, at least in the beginning. You would go to bed one night and wake up the next morning unable to walk. Paralyzed! It was believed that swimming pools might harbor the germ that could infect us, so public pools were closed. Perhaps the Ritz picture show was closed too; I don't remember. One summer, probably about 1947 when I was eight years old, there were more polio cases than ever. We lived with a feeling of terror and dread. Was this germ in the air, could it travel from person to person, who next would be paralyzed? It seemed that children were particularly at risk, so we attempted to avoid crowds as much as possible.

That summer I spent much of my time at my friend Gail's

house. Looking back on that time, I don't know if this was a conscious effort on the part of our families to try to keep us both away from crowds. (If I had been with my parents, I would have been at our store where there was always a crowd. Since Gail lived just outside the city, her playmates were always "imported." So, this worked out well for Gail and for me.) My being at Gail's house was real luxury. As an example of this luxury, her mother made our breakfast every morning, whereas at my house you often made your own. I soon discovered the joy of lying in the first hammock I had ever experienced, and Gail had records that did not just play music but actually featured someone telling fascinating stories for children. But our fun didn't end there. Some of the activities I recall were playing dress-up with old curtains under their Mulberry tree, creating artworks using Gail's many molds in the sand box, and—most exciting of all—riding Lucky. This was Gail's little Shetland pony that frightened me, yet I loved riding him.

But what was really important at Gail's house was the bath after lunch and rest. The thought was that we should not become overly tired, since this might weaken our resistance to the polio germ and we might "GET IT!" After our baths, we would lie in bed and read comic books and discuss the fun we just had and make plans for more fun. All this got me through the summer, and I almost forgot about the polio danger since Gail and her mother made avoiding polio so special.

Only when we went back to school in the fall did we hear

about a student two years older than we were who actually got polio. When this girl did return to school, she had a limp, and over the years her leg atrophied. However, the worst sight I remember was seeing another girl who had polio lying in an iron lung. I don't recall if my class went to this most disturbing viewing or if I went with my family or friends out of curiosity. Probably the intentions by the medical community were good. Maybe they hoped to raise money for research about polio or to educate the public. No matter the reason, however, even I at age eight realized it was a sideshow. I don't think this kind of exploitation could happen today, at least I hope not.

This is what I saw. A bus-like vehicle had been driven into town and was parked on our Main Street. Anyone curious about polio could enter through the vehicle's front door. I was curious, as were many other people. We entered the bus, first encountering unusual objects of cold steel, tubes, and glass. This was 1940s medical technology that looked like gadgets in a Frankenstein movie. Then, in the midst of all of this hardware, we saw a thin, pale girl lying in what appeared to be a metal-and-glass coffin, with her head sticking out. To make her feel better (I guess), a mirror was placed over her head so she could see behind her or to the side. This "coffin" was called an "iron lung." Without it, she could not breathe and would die. I somehow realized that she had to get out of this horrible but life-saving contraption sometimes, since she was dressed in pajamas. There was a nurse standing next to her explaining the circumstances of this girl and giving us more information about polio. I have to admit that I heard nothing but unintelligible sounds coming from the "nurse-educator's" mouth. I just wanted to get out of there. I tried to find a place to look that was not disturbing. My eyes went to the mirror and there were the girl's eyes looking back at me. I think I felt the full meaning of shame for the first time in my memory. I wanted to say to her, "I'm so sorry you have polio, and I'm so sorry to be here staring at you." I bowed my head, evading her eyes, and then (mercifully) we were instructed to depart the vehicle through the back door.

Each year there were more and more cases of polio, with 1952 being the worst epidemic year. The vaccine developed by Dr. Jonas Salk was available on a limited basis in 1953 and by 1955 it was available for the masses. I would be seventeen before I felt safe from the disease.

THE BIGGEST WORRY OF ALL

WAR WAS MY GREATEST WORRY OF ALL AS A CHILD. My earliest memories are of war. I was almost one year old when World War II began and six (almost seven) years old when it ended in 1945. During these formative years of childhood, we all worked to help "The Cause." We children contributed by scouring the rock roads and ditches for bits of tinfoil to collect and save for the war effort. We tried not to complain when deprived of sugar, since it was rationed, and we wasted nothing. People didn't just have gardens; they had "Victory Gardens" to help with the scarcity of food. Everything was needed for our troops and we supported them. "The Cause" was noble.

My closest relative in the war was my mother's younger brother, Lamar Edwards. I assume he was one of the ten million young men drafted into the war—or it is possible he volunteered. I don't know to this day. Maybe the posters with Uncle Sam looking directly at him and pointing his finger, saying *"I want you"* convinced Uncle Lamar to go. In a large canvas bag, my grandmother, Mama Edwards, collected and saved all of Lamar's letters written to Papa

Edwards and to her. I can still see this bag hanging from a big nail that was driven right into the wall of their home. My grandmother allowed me to take these precious letters and put them against the glass window where the sun shone through them. On top of Lamar's letters, I laid a clean sheet of writing paper and traced them, copying each line as he had written it. I was not able to read one word of it, since at that time I was just learning to print. I don't know who came up with this activity for me, but it was one of my favorite things to do. I have thought about my uncle's war letters over the years and have wondered what happened to them. How I wish I still had Lamar's letters and my copies of them.

Most of our large family meals back then were at my grandparents' house, and our main topic of conversation was, of course, the war. Because Lamar was in the Pacific in the U.S. Navy on a large aircraft carrier, the USS Franklin, war for me was more at sea and with the Japanese. I would get confused about the Germans and Europe, but it seemed the whole world was in flames. There were children starving, people being tortured, and bombs exploding. The worry of when all this madness would end was of concern for everyone. Even when I went to a picture show I was exposed to newsreels that graphically showed the fighting. When these horrific scenes of reality ended, a cartoon often featuring the popular trickster, Bugs Bunny, came on the screen. It was as if our minds were being jerked from one pole to the other.

My childhood worries were magnified when my family moved

to Blytheville, where there was a large advanced flying school training base about five miles from our house. Planes were flying in and out all of the time. It was the noise of war. At the end of my street there stood a magnificent Indian mound and, just beyond this mound, runways had been built for the planes. When I thought it couldn't get much worse, a prisoner-of-war camp for Germans captured in Europe was erected amidst this mix of war, planes, and the Indian mound. Now the war with the Germans became more real to me, since the prisoners were now my neighbors! Thinking back on this time, it all now seems rather insane.

Because our men had gone to war "over there," we did not have sufficient labor needed to farm our cotton. But being ever resourceful, our government came up with a plan to have prisoners-of-war provide desperately needed labor. Did you know the U.S. had Nazis hoeing and picking American cotton? But the program became complicated, overregulated, and caused unexpected and unintended consequences. I have read little about this interesting slice of history; but let me be quick to add that as far as I know the German and a few Italian prisoners were paid a wage and the number of hours they worked was limited by the Geneva Convention.

The worst nightmare I recall from those days was about a fire started by the Germans at the prisoner-of-war camp. In my dream, the fire slowly crept block by block from the camp and came toward my house, engulfing grassy lawns, shrubbery, trees, and our neighbors' homes. I stood silently at my bedroom window, spellbound by the enormity and hopelessness of it. The flames drew closer and closer to our house and then began to lick up the wall beneath my window. I continued to watch the enemy fire, waiting to be burned alive, when—mercifully—I awoke. That dream has stayed with me for the last seventy-four years.

My Uncle Lamar was not as lucky as I was; he lived this nightmare. His ship—loaded with 36,000 gallons of fuel, over 50 planes loaded with fuel and bombs, as well as 30 tons of bombs stored on deck—was hit by Japanese *"kamikaze"* planes. Only in 2014 was there finally a documentary produced, "USS Franklin: Honor Restored," narrated by Captain Dale Dye and directed by Robert Childs, that described this catastrophe. According to the documentary, the skipper of the USS Franklin was an arrogant and disliked man who had mental issues. The men on the ship were put in harm's way by his inability to make good decisions. The documentary uses actual archival footage and interviews about this horrific event. Lamar was badly burned and tossed into the sea. After hours in the cold water, he was rescued by a plane, but then it crashed. Lamar was again rescued and taken to Tasmania, off the coast of Australia, where a talented surgeon was able to miraculously put my uncle's handsome face back together. Before Lamar returned home, we children were given strict orders to never ever ask him about the war. And we did not.

Just about a year before Lamar died in 1999, however, when

he was 76 years old, I disobeyed this long-standing family policy. For the first time, I asked him to tell me about his experiences in the war. I took some notes about his story and incredible rescue. Out of the 3,000 men on the ship that day, about 800 were killed and almost 500 were wounded. As Lamar and I talked, his wife, Bea, left the room. I was thinking maybe his story was too much for her to hear, but when she returned, she was holding a beautiful box and said to me, "I thought you might want to see this." In the box was Lamar's Purple Heart, which I never knew he had received and obviously had never seen. Silently, Uncle Lamar looked at me. It was as if, after all these years, he had been waiting for someone to ask him to tell his story.

EASTER, 4ᵀᴴ OF JULY, AND THANKSGIVING

EASTER

FAMILY AND TRADITIONS IN NORTHEASTERN ARKANSAS went hand and hand in the 1940s and 1950s. As a child, it seemed to me it would always be so, but that did not turn out to be completely true. In our extended family, we celebrated four major holidays. No matter the state of our country or economy, we celebrated Easter, 4th of July, Thanksgiving, and—the best of all—Christmas.

Easter, of course, was about Jesus overcoming death (we all knew that), but to put a happy spin on it we put fun into Easter by having lots of Easter-egg hunts. I think deep down, by the age of six or seven at least, we kids all knew these eggs were not laid (hard-boiled, colored, and hidden on our lawn overnight, no less) by some miraculous rabbit. Most of the eggs were dyed one simple color, but for some fortunate children with artistic parents (not mine) the eggs were two-toned or even three-toned, sort of mimicking the coloring of cars at that time. But even if, and eventually when, we learned the truth about the bunny, no child wanted to admit it, since that meant the fun would end for everyone. So, bright and early every Easter Sunday morning (even before church services) we four Byrd children dashed out of the door into our backyard with baskets in tow to hunt for the eggs that the miraculous bunny always left during the night.

Naturally, Easter Sunday was also the big church-going day of the year. This always called for new clothes, including hats, gloves, shoes, purses, and dresses for the girls (and of course, a new suit for our brother Don). I can imagine the pressure my mother must have felt getting all of these outfits together for all four children, and of course her own ensemble, while working full time at our store. (Daddy never seemed to care much about his clothes, but even he would put on a new shirt and tie for Easter.) However, retailers knew of the "Southern Easter Sunday" outfit clothing tradition, so Mother probably could find many "matching" outfits already created by enterprising shopkeepers, especially after we moved to Blytheville. To set our outfits off, we girls and our mother received corsages from the florist that had been ordered earlier in the week and were delivered that morning just before church and Sunday school. (Even as an adult, I never feel "right" not wearing fresh flowers on Easter Sunday.)

Although it may seem shocking now in our more secular society, but during this period of America's history even our public schools celebrated Easter if they chose to. It was different each year, but the best celebration I remember was the year we had an Easter-egg hunt in Blytheville's Walker Park. There were three grade schools in our town at the time, and this hunt was exclusively for all fourth graders, of which I was one. This was the first time I remembered all three schools coming together for an event. Prior to the hunt, we were shown the prize for the most eggs found. It was a huge, golden, sparkly egg with a glass window you could peer into to see a three-dimensional diorama depicting an idyllic formal garden scene.

I really wanted to win that egg! But so did all the other kids. We were given an entire hour to run around and hunt for the literally hundreds of eggs that had been hidden by the adults. Truly we must have looked rather comical running in every direction, overturning large fallen limbs of trees, walking through piles of dead branches, pushing mounds of leaves aside, and looking under and around anything that might hide an egg. (It never occurred to me until years later that snakes were probably emerging from their winter dormant state that day.) I don't even remember being with my friends during this search. It was every girl and boy for herself or himself.

For the sake of this story I would like to say I found the most eggs, received the golden egg and lived happily ever after. But the most eggs were found by a boy named Jack, who wasn't even in our class at Central but was from one of the *other* schools. We all began to get over our disappointment as we gathered after the hunt in the Girl Scout House on the park property. Here we continued to socialize with our old and now new friends, drinking punch and devouring cookies. Jack walked about the large room (showing off we thought) with the golden egg in his outstretched arm and hand for all to see. Although we felt he was taunting us, in hindsight I admit that the green-eyed monster of jealousy had us losers in its grip. To Jack's credit he allowed us to peer into the egg and view the idyllic scene as much as we wanted, and we began to soften our feelings towards him. For days after returning to school, we talked about the fun we had on our big Easter-egg hunt in the spring of 1949.

So, if my present and future family members want to understand why I continue to sponsor Easter-egg hunts for my grown grandchildren and their spouses and friends and all their kids, it is to share with them some of the joy I felt from the camaraderie from Easters long ago. I hope good and happy memories and family traditions are being created for them.

4TH OF JULY

INDEPENDENCE DAY, WHICH HAS ALWAYS BEEN CELEBRATED on July 4th since the time of our founders, took on a totally different feeling from our Easter traditions. These were, in my not-so-humble childhood opinion, the best celebrations (except for Christmas) my grandmother, Mama Edwards, organized every year. I have no photographs of how our Arkansas July 4th celebration looked, but if

Norman Rockwell had seen it, he most certainly would have painted it. The setting was usually outside among the willow trees at my grandparents' home, with tables comprised of Papa Edwards' sawhorses with big sheets of plywood laid over them. Mama Edwards (as everyone called her) would then put cotton tablecloths in a variety of patterns over the plywood. Nothing matched.

Cars and truckloads of our relatives arrived, carrying food they brought to add to the celebration. Earlier in the day, my daddy had made the ice cream and had it ready to be churned in the hand-cranked freezers. While the women were preparing the food and setting the tables, Daddy (aka "the ice-cream chef") was organizing his army of helpers for this task. At least three hand-turned ice cream makers/freezers were going at a time, with all the kids begging for a turn at the crank. When we could no longer turn the crank, we knew the cream had hardened. It was time to remove the dashers (the dasher is a paddle-like instrument that stirs the ice cream, ensuring that it freezes uniformly) from the canisters. Of course, we children would argue over who would get to lick the fast melting cream from each dasher. The canisters now only contained our heavenly treat, but it was not yet to be eaten. The canisters' lids were secured, and then around each canister we packed more rock salt and ice, pushing it firm between the canister and the wall of its maker/freezer. On top of this whole contraption, blankets were placed to "hold in" the cold.

As the ice cream further hardened, we kids gathered at the

great makeshift tables in a group and the adults gravitated to other tables. It was fun over the years to watch a few of the older cousins trying to decide with which group they should sit. Someone always said a blessing, and then we enjoyed our meal together. There was the usual fare of corn on the cob, barbecued beef, fried chicken, homegrown sliced tomatoes, cornbread, giant yeast rolls that only Mama Edwards could make, watermelon, cantaloupe, cucumber pickles, sweet tea and more. We never ate from paper or plastic ware—even if such a thing existed back then. The dishes, in other words, were as real as the food. No additives touched our lips; all food was grown or raised on our farms and served fresh to us while we sat under the willows.

Perhaps because the 4th of July was about our War of Independence from the British, this holiday always seemed to stimulate war conversations. As years passed at our family's gathering, so did the wars. World War II was definitely the worst war in our minds, but after it ended, we entered into the Korean War and then the Cold War with the Russians. The talk of the atomic bomb penetrated our conversations, and then the terrifying hydrogen bomb was developed. Much uncertainty surrounded the hydrogen bomb, especially since for a while there was actual fear of one of them igniting the air and destroying us all. We all believed our country was good and protected by God, so I guess after years of hearing about war we began to accept it as a natural part of life.

But not all July 4th conversation was of doom and gloom. How could it be, as it was served up with great food and delightful, fun, and loving cousins who were eager to play? My favorite cousin, Mary Esther, and I always agreed on what was fun and inventive. On one 4th of July we made ourselves "hula skirts" like those the girls were wearing in a picture with our Uncle Lamar, who was serving in the Pacific. He was standing there wearing his sailor uniform with a big smile on his face while being surrounded by these exotic girls. It didn't take us long to make our own grass skirts out of the willows. All we knew about Hawaii was that the war started there for America and that they had "hula girls." Our imitation of the "hula" was based entirely on what we had seen in newsreels at the picture show. This reenactment was just one of the many performance pieces Mary Esther and I created over the years. But the best of our celebration was yet to come. As it grew dark and the country sky was radiant with stars, the long-awaited homemade ice cream was released from its cold cave and, as usual, we all agreed it was the best ice cream served on Earth.

Then to complete the evening and our celebration, my brother, Don, and I put on a firework's show, loosely supervised by our daddy. This show was absolutely nothing as grand as fireworks people see now days, but we would bring firecrackers, sparklers, Devil chasers, and Roman candles from our store. Our favorites were the Devil chasers since you really never knew which direction these "fire demons" would race over the ground. They had everyone running, and then when they stopped their run—they exploded. I don't think Devil chasers stayed on the market too long since they were very dangerous.

Mother refused to even hold an unlit Roman candle ever since one had backfired on her once and the fire balls had raced down her arm. (To be honest, I always thought Mother had simply held the Roman candle upside down, but it never seemed to be the right time for me to bring this up to her.)

The sparklers were like magic to us kids. We ran as fast as we could in a long line following the leader and creating a brilliant line of light. In retrospect, it was only a miracle that Don, who had no discernment about danger and absolutely no fear, did not lose a hand with the firecrackers. And it still amazes me that the adults gave us kids so much freedom—but, hey, isn't that what July 4th represents?

THANKSGIVING

I ALWAYS FELT THAT THANKSGIVING was just a "warm-up" to Christmas. We (meaning my immediate family, cousins, aunts and uncles) gathered, as was our tradition, at Papa and Mama Edwards' house. The food was bountiful, and the center of attention was always the giant turkey with sage dressing, which would be reprised in a few weeks when we all gathered again for Christmas, but with the much-anticipated addition of presents!

Thanksgiving was a time to stuff ourselves, and one year that is what I literally did. I was challenged by Uncle Lamar to eat everything on my plate that I had piled high, resembling a small mountain of food. He said I couldn't do it. Well, you know what that meant. I was determined to do it, no matter the risk to my stomach. I stuffed myself and acted as if I relished every bite. The last few bites were hard to swallow, but I "won" the challenge. When I finished all the food, Lamar nonchalantly said, "Oh, that's good." That was that. His response was so cavalier. That is when the light bulb came on in my head. He had manipulated me again. I may have won, but I felt terrible for several hours. As usual I was the butt of someone's joke! Fortunately, I soon recovered and was able to laugh. Deep down I believed that Lamar picked on me because I was his favorite niece, and he definitely was my favorite uncle.

After our Thanksgiving meal our parents always sent us outside to play. The late November days were usually cold, and we children had a lot of pent-up energy. But our outside play never lasted very long. Certainly not long enough for our parents. The adults would linger around the table discussing the war and the recent cotton crop. We children would find activities to pass the time. Playing with a feather mattress would always keep us entertained for a while. It took about six of us to grasp the edges of the mattress and heave it up and down to fluff it. We would carefully lay it in place on the bed and then take turns jumping into the center of it, sinking into the soft and gentle hug that enveloped our bodies. After tiring of this game, we would crank up my grandparents' old Victrola and put on a well-worn phonograph record. It sounded, honestly, as if someone were in a box and surrounded by tin, but it pleased us kids as we danced and sang along. Then, as the day wore on, we often pulled out old photos and tried to identify family and friends. I remember lying on my grandmother's bed with my dearest cousin, Mary Esther, looking at these pictures, thinking that family gatherings like this would go on forever. It was such an ordinary part of my life for so many years that I did not realize the subtle changes occurring each year were foretelling a future without these traditions.

Prior to the family event, Thanksgiving at school was celebrated as well. This usually meant our class performed for the Rotary Club or another service organization. We dressed like pilgrims in the paper hats and collars we made in class and sang traditional songs such as, "Faith of our Fathers," "We Gather Together," and "America the Beautiful." Loving God and country were accepted in Arkansas by both our families and our schools; they gave purpose, continuity, and harmony to our lives.

MAIN STREET, PARADES, AND CHURCH NATIVITY SCENE

MAIN STREET

THERE IS USUALLY A MAIN STREET IN EVERY SMALL TOWN. Growing up before anyone thought up the idea of Walmart or even a mall, I thought Main Street was not only the place for commerce, it was also a place to see or be seen by a friend or neighbor.

For us in Blytheville, and maybe other towns as well, Christmas transformed Main Street into a magical wonderland-like place. Shop windows were cleaned to display the latest toys, appliances, or "have to have" gifts for the holidays. The sparkly shop windows were edged in sprayed-on snow, colorful lights, and large letters wishing passersby "Merry Christmas." Shop doors tinkled with the sound of bells when customers entered, and a familiar shopkeeper greeted us when we walked into each store. If you think of today's Hallmark television network's Christmas shows, you get the picture. Whoever writes those simple, feel good, always happy-ending shows, must have visited Blytheville at Christmastime.

The entire city decorated itself as if it were one big home or school. Large, fat garlands were strung above our heads, from one side of Main to the other, as far as the eye could see. In the middle of these garlands were huge bells that made no sound but seemed ready to chime at any moment. Loudspeakers set along Main Street heightened our awareness of the celebration of the season. I never tired of my favorite cowboy, Gene Autry, singing, "Here Comes Santa Claus" or "Rudolph the Red Nose Reindeer." Thinking about the canned music now, I chuckle to myself when I remember how excited I would get when my parents would say, "Let's drive down to Main Street and listen to the Christmas music and watch the shoppers." All six us of would pack into our Chevrolet (later Oldsmobile) and go downtown.

After the car was parked, our parents would remember they had to go "check" on something in one of the shops. They would leave us sitting in the car. Yes, sitting by ourselves! We kids were a contented lot—seeing folks we knew, saying "hey," and listening to the music. And if the miracles of miracles occurred, we might get to see a bit of snow. When the snow fell, and it did sometimes, there was no place on earth more beautiful to me at that moment.

Years later, after I was married, my husband's work gave us opportunities to live in Europe and travel to some great cities. When we visited these famous places at Christmas time, I always appreciated their beautiful decorations and customs. Some of my travels included: Berlin with incredible decorations, Madrid's spectacular

"Three Kings Parade" on the eve of Epiphany, and decorated Christmas windows of the famous department stores, Marshall Fields in Chicago and Lord and Taylor in New York. I still consider Christmas on Main Street in Blytheville, Arkansas, to be the best.

PARADES

THE CHRISTMAS PARADE IN BLYTHEVILLE was just one of many parades on Main Street throughout the year. Certainly, one of our most important parades was held on October 6, 1945, when President Harry Truman waved to us from his open-air convertible as he rode down our Main Street. This was so special that my parents made sure our entire family witnessed this bit of history. Another celebrity who waved to us with a special turn of her hand as she sat, like a queen, high in a convertible, was Rebecca McCall of Blytheville. In 1946, she had just missed being named Miss America and returned triumphantly in a parade through Blytheville as the first runner-up. She was still a winner to all of us in Blytheville.

There were smaller parades before homecoming football games, and each fall we celebrated Blytheville's important National Cotton Picking Contest with a huge parade. Of course, being a town that respected the soldiers who protected our country, there were many, many parades held to honor our military. Sometimes even I thought folks just wanted to have another parade.

But as far as I was concerned, the Christmas parade each year was the best of all, and one in particular, in 1949, even included a little danger which, as you know by now, was my favorite thing as a young girl. My Girl Scout Troop had been invited to participate in the Christmas parade, and someone proposed the idea that we have a single scout out in front of our float, holding onto a great silver cord and pretending to pull the float down the street. The words had no sooner left our scout leader's mouth when my hand shot up volunteering to be this girl. No one else had a chance to volunteer, even if she wanted to, although I think no one wanted to.

When my parents heard this news, of course, they were not pleased. They were concerned that I would be no more than a few feet in front of the truck that housed the float and could easily be run over if I wasn't careful. In other words, my life would be in the hands of the man who drove the truck behind me. Who was this man driving the truck, my parents demanded to know, or was it just a kid? Since anyone could get a driver's license in Arkansas at age 14 at the time, it was a distinct possibility a young inexperienced person could be the driver. Well, how exciting was this! So much drama, and I would be at the center of it. Although my parents had shown little concern for me as I ran about the countryside at Mandalay, they were now showing unusual concern for my safety, and I found this confusing. I never heard so many questions from them. In addition to the safety issue, they were concerned that I would have to walk for two or three miles in the cold weather down Main

Street. (I had experienced a rough time with my health when I was five and six years old, but that was ancient history as far as I was concerned.) I was within a few days of being eleven, practically a teenager.

In the end, I was allowed to "pull" the float, but my parents bought an assortment of warm undergarments that they forced me to wear. Honestly, I was dressed like a duck hunter. It was difficult to get my scout uniform over all the padding.

I remember Daddy "talking" to the (turned out to be) mature man who would be driving the truck for the float, making sure that the silver cord was several yards long and that I would be far away from the front of the truck. It was an exhilarating moment as I hoisted the great silver cord (here I have to tell the truth, in reality it was just a cheap thin silver Christmas garland) over my shoulder and walked the length of Main Street, pretending with all the theatrics I could muster that I was indeed pulling a heavy load. Somewhere down deep inside, I appreciated the concern my parents had shown, although earlier it had annoyed me. But to be on the safe side, I often glanced over my shoulder as I walked proudly pulling the float. As Ronald Reagan said to the Russians decades later, quoting an old Russian proverb: "Trust but verify."

CHURCH NATIVITY SCENE

THE FIRST METHODIST CHURCH (now the First United Methodist Church) situated on Main Street in Blytheville still stands as it did when I attended there as a child. Forever implanted in my mind is the architecture of this church. I cannot erase what has become for me the way a church should look. Every church I have attended as an adult I have measured against this strong, dignified, stained-glass, cathedral-like structure. Nowadays, many church buildings have become places for performances, and the grandeur of the Gothic arches that rose to the heavens that I cherished as a child are long gone. Yes, times do change, and I know God is more than a building, but still—my memories of First Methodist do linger. Christmastime at this church was what one would expect: It was all about the birth of Jesus. One Christmas it was decided we would have a live Nativity scene on the lawn in front of the church. This plan caused a bit of commotion among all the Sunday-school classes. We had many eager children who wanted to be part of this performance, and it must have taken a master scheduler to ensure that all who wanted to participate could have a role and that no one was slighted. The reenactment would be continuous for the week before Christmas, for one hour every night. Each child would participate in fifteen-minute shifts. Spotlights remained focused on the scene and, very fortunately, a doll was used for baby Jesus. The manger was built, costumes (someone's bath robe, I suspect) were issued, props such as a shepherd's crook appeared, and the wise men looked royal. Appropriately dressed in a white flowing gown sprinkled with glitter, an angel hovered close to Mary and Joseph as they knelt by the manger. Living in a farming community, it wasn't difficult to round up a few sheep. The whole thing was simple and stunning.

I remember the night of my "performance" was cold but not bitter. The quietness of the evening felt holy. I could feel the cold earth pressing against my knees, even though padding had been placed there to protect me. We were instructed not to talk or move about, but rather to hold still as if we were sculptures. Cars drove slowly down Main Street past our little scene. It was the only time I ever had the privilege to portray Mary, and I keep this as one of my best Christmas memories.

CHRISTMAS AT HOME AND IN SCHOOL

AT HOME

CHRISTMAS TREES IN ARKANSAS WERE SLIM PICKINGS. Growing up in the northeastern part of Arkansas, I never saw or heard of a Christmas tree farm. We only grew cotton on our farms! To my knowledge I never saw a fir, pine, or spruce tree unless it was shipped into our area at Christmas time. I was told that these usually scrawny, misshaped, puny little trees came from "up north," which meant Missouri to me. But what is fascinating, I think, is that—after we decorated a tree with old ornaments and bubble lights that we pulled from the back of the closet each year—the tree took on its own festive and familiar personality. Of course, we could never load it down with enough aluminum icicles. The icicles were the icing on the cake or, I should say, on the tree. I have reflected on why we smothered the tree with so many aluminum icicles, and I suppose it was to hide some of the tree's flaws, or perhaps my parents found it added to the holiday mood, or maybe because the icicles were so inexpensive that nobody cared and it kept us kids quiet for hours. I have wondered if—in some bizarre way—this practice influenced Mother to purchase the aluminum tree that suddenly and inexplicably appeared later in my life. Anyway, after the tree was decorated, Daddy and the interested kids in the family, and maybe a friend or two, would walk across the street and look back at our house with the tree bubbling bright in front of our picture window. We always agreed that this tree was the best one we had ever had.

A group of my friends and I and our mothers held an elegant Christmas party every year for seven years when we girls were ages seven to thirteen. Three girls of this small group have remained my lifelong friends. We used fine china, silverware, and crystal glasses, as well as our best manners at the party. We all (daughters and mothers alike) wore our new Christmas dresses and looked forward to this yearly Christmas event, which rotated from home to home. I guess this story is important to me because I believe friendships and manners matter. We may have been from Arkansas, but we considered ourselves to be part of polite society.

The year when it was my turn to have the party at our house in Blytheville, my mother decided to have it on my twelfth birthday and celebrate my birthday along with the elegant Christmas soiree. It was one of the most important parties of my young life. A picture was taken by a professional who came to the house and took pictures, including a picture of my friends and me gathered around the Christmas tree.

Years later, when inspecting that picture, I noticed the icicle-laden Christmas tree at the center of the party. It was bushy, misshapen, and rather pitiful, like an alien intruder who hogged the picture. On top, or I should say *almost* on top of the tree was an "angel" sitting cockeyed in a way that defied gravity. She had a big, fat, white electrical cord that ran from "her" down the front and center of the tree. There had been no effort to hide the cord among the tree's branches. (Obviously esthetics were not a strong suit with my family, but at least the person who took the photo didn't capture the reproductions of "Pinkie" and "Blue Boy" that were on the wall above the sofa just out of range of the camera.)*

This memorable party remains one of my happiest memories because it was the only organized birthday celebration I ever had as a child. Because my birthday is on December 22, it always occurs exactly three days before Christmas Day and therefore was always overshadowed by Jesus' birthday—or at least that was what my friends thought. But my experience has been just the opposite: My birthday is easy for friends and family to remember precisely because it is just before Christmas, so actually it was seldom overlooked. Just ask my husband... and my children...and my grandchildren!

On this particular birthday of mine, in 1950, my friend Nelia Woods' mother, Opal Woods, made the infamous Hundred Dollar

---

* *For those of another generation, I feel an explanation is needed. "Pinkie" was painted by Thomas Lawrence in 1794 and "Blue Boy" was painted by Thomas Gainsborough in 1770. They were both reproduced countless times and in the 1950s became the icons of culture in middle-class homes, at least in Arkansas: Pinkie dressed in pink and Blue Boy dressed in blue.*

Cake for my party. The recipe originated with a famous chef of the Waldorf Astoria in New York. Now, we may have lived in Arkansas, but we knew the Waldorf Astoria. The story is that the chef at the Waldorf received a letter from a woman who had enjoyed the cake while staying at the hotel. She asked for the recipe, and the chef sent her the recipe along with an invoice for a hundred dollars! The woman was so incensed by the bill that she retaliated by having the recipe printed in several magazines. There was a legal battle, but the woman won. She *had* paid for the recipe, the court ruled. Thus, it became The Hundred Dollar Cake. The cake was, and still is, delicious, and I have included the recipe in the back of this book.

IN SCHOOL

IF CHRISTMAS AT HOME WAS A TIME FOR CELEBRATION, our schools multiplied the tradition by honoring this joyous season as well. Each year, teachers were at liberty to decide how their classrooms would be decorated and what special programs would be presented. It was always a highly anticipated occasion as we students took part in transforming our classroom with colors of red and green as we created scenes of winter and Christmas.

On this particular Christmas we all had reason to celebrate, since Japan had surrendered in September of 1945, ending six long years of war. Our spirits were lifted and hope was everywhere. Mr. Charles Hindman, our neighbor and a wholesaler for our store, wanted to acknowledge this auspicious event and Christmas, as well; he surprised our school with a Christmas tree for every room. His entrance into the school with the six trees was accompanied by the delicious fresh smell of pine and lots of laughter. It was obvious that his giving made him as happy as it made my classmates and teachers. We immediately set about making colorful paper chains from construction paper for the tree's decoration.

The fresh smell of pine lingered in our room all week, and then gifts began to appear under the tree for our teacher. It was a tradition to give the teachers a Christmas present. The gifts were never extravagant, but rather small, useful things, perhaps even something our teachers might use in the classroom.

Although the war had ended three months prior to the Christmas celebration in my second 1st grade, many goods were still scarce. In fact, it was 1947 before rationing ended on sugar. Orange juice was still difficult to find, but somehow my parents found six one-gallon cans of this precious liquid gold: one gallon for each teacher. How Mother and Daddy managed to place a gallon under each Christmas tree in each class, I don't know, but they did. What I do remember most vividly is seeing my teacher, Mrs. Willoughby, tear back the thin tissue paper around the can of juice and scream with glee. She grabbed the can and ran to the classroom next door, where that teacher had just opened her gift of juice. Throughout the school, teachers were running from room to room, laughing and shouting with delight about their good fortune in receiving such a precious and unexpected gift.

Yes, Christmas at school taught us children a lot: share what we had, work together, and respect our teachers. Christmas was good at Blytheville Central Elementary Grade School.

CHRISTMAS AT THE STORE, IN FLORIDA, AND OVER FAMILY DINNERS

AT THE STORE

I ALWAYS KNEW IT WAS GETTING CLOSE TO CHRISTMAS because the signs were all around me: The sun took a holiday; the gray skies moved in; the last of the cotton was picked. Now in its place were big, dark, craggy sticks standing in untidy rows jutting from the black ground. The chug, chug, chug of the cotton gin's giant motor had fallen silent.

How I loved autumn in Arkansas! The cold and gray of November and December were tolerable only because Christmas was coming and my favorite display in our store was about to reappear.

The merchandise in one particular area of our store always reflected the season. During spring and summer big canvas cotton-picking sacks, hoes, work gloves, seeds and other objects for gardening and farming were displayed. The inventory of these items became quite small as fall approached, and then suddenly not one of these items remained on the floor. Seemingly overnight, all the farming stuff had been swept away—really, they disappeared—and a plethora of toys and Christmas gifts took their place. For a kid (particularly one stuck in the middle of a cotton field) this was about as close as you could get to Heaven on Earth. Naturally there were dolls, stuffed animals, piggy banks, the usual. But what I begged for, and could not stop talking about, was a BB gun. I'm totally serious. The 1983 movie *A Christmas Story* (which was set in the 1940s that I am describing here) has several scenes where the main character's mother and teacher both warn him: "You'll shoot your eye out." This was my story. I was a female Ralphie!

In fact, these were the exact words my mother said to me; but it was my obsession just as it was for Ralphie in the movie. I could not let it go. Honestly, it was as if a spotlight had been put on those BB guns as they were displayed in our store each Christmas season for several years. I think I was twelve years old before I finally broke my parents down and they gave me a BB gun. It was a genuine Daisy Red Ryder, based on the comic book and Western film character, Red Ryder. My sister Bob says I was only nine or ten when I got the gun, and maybe she is right. It seemed that I waited my whole childhood to get my first gun, so you'll have to excuse me if I get the chronology a bit wrong. (For the record, I never did come close to shooting my eye out. Of course, my reckless brother, Don, almost shot my eye out, but fortunately the glass window of the car I was in saved me. But that is a story for another book.)

It wasn't just toys that made our Christmas display special; it was also the new and enticing foods that only appeared in the store at this time of year. Unlike today, when we can buy almost any food at any time no matter the season in large supermarkets or big-box stores or even online, such was not the case in the 1940s. We ate what was in season. At our store, my parents brought in these seasonal food items, but they also imported some exotic treats.

I remember vividly these tasty foods: big, sweet oranges from Florida; colorful ribbons made of candy; fancy boxes of chocolate-covered cherries; hairy, round, brown coconuts; large, hard Brazil nuts; precious dates; bright-yellow bananas still hanging from their stalk; and luscious chocolate and coconut cakes from a bakery in Blytheville. These cakes were decorated with edible miniature Christmas wreaths or poinsettias made of hard sugar in the red and green colors of the Christmas season. One of the truly spectacular treats was a huge wheel of sharp cheddar cheese that we called "rat cheese." The cheese arrived in a wooden box built specifically for the cheese. And it came from *Europe*—no small feat during the war and even after it ended. In fact, many of our store's mysterious foods came from other countries and far away states. (How ironic that today we consider ourselves lucky to find locally grown food among all the imported food on the shelves of many stores.)

This Christmas tradition continued for about ten to fifteen years at our store. Toys and food changed as our society changed, of course, and especially after the large rural-agrarian society I grew up in began to migrate to urban areas. We now had better roads, cars were affordable for the masses, and farmers used bigger machines and developed better technology for growing things. Fewer people were needed to farm or live on farms. As Bob Dylan put it in 1964, the times certainly were a-changin'.

IN FLORIDA

When I was about eight or nine years old, my parents mentioned a word that had never been part of their vocabulary. That word was "vacation." They told their four children that they had not closed the store, except for Sundays and Christmas Day, for over ten years and had decided we all deserved a vacation, which meant a trip to that far-away, exotic land of Florida. (This was a time when we had sufficient experienced help to run the store, and my parents felt comfortable leaving their responsibilities behind during the slower business and farming times. The store would remain open, but it would be left in the "safe hands" of longtime employees Mr. Homer and Miss Hollis for about two weeks.)

So, for many years right after Christmas Mother and Daddy took the family to Florida for about ten days. I finally saw orange groves where our Christmas oranges grew and sampled fresh orange juice from roadside stands that were sprinkled along the new 1940s highway. In Florida I discovered shrimp, flounder, and other food stuff of the ocean that we never "carried" in our store. I loved our winter vacations at the ocean and in the historic town of St. Augustine. I remember Mother wanted to find the Fountain of Youth (supposedly) discovered there by Ponce de Leon. It was strange not to be surrounded by cotton stalks and the cold, gray Arkansas days, but I knew that no matter how comfortable and exciting Florida was, with all its new sights and experiences, I would always return to the cotton fields of white gold and our home in Blytheville.

OVER FAMILY DINNERS

THE REALLY BIG OCCASION OF THE YEAR for our extended family was our Christmas dinner. We shared the bounty from our store, and Mama Edwards pulled out all the stops. These Christmas gatherings were never about the gifts. Santa had already delivered them earlier Christmas morning to our house, and we arrived at Papa and Mama Edwards' house with our arms tightly wrapped around many new toys we would share in play with our cousins.

We always brought a small gift for Mama Edwards that usually reflected the popular costume jewelry of the season, since we knew she liked the gaudy, colorful stones. For Papa we would bring new tobacco for his pipe and maybe even a new pipe. Decorations in our grandparents' house were minimal, but at Christmas there was always cheer in the air and a spirit unlike our other family gatherings. Christmas was about being together as a family, laughing and talking with one another, and enjoying delicious food. Simple, huh?

No need to complicate it.

We kids adored our Arkansas cousins, of course, so we played together without arguing as we enjoyed our new toys. Our cousins were a most agreeable bunch and there were usually about twenty of us gathered around two tables. The children sat together, not feeling for one minute that we had been banished to the kitchen. We saw this as a bonus since we could "carry on" with no adults to supervise. (During the war years it was a relief to sit away from the adults, since meal conversation was focused on the current fighting. I think they thought we were not listening—but we were.)

Christmas dinner was Thanksgiving dinner on steroids. A huge turkey with cornbread dressing was the center attraction. We never put oysters in the dressing as some southerners did. We liked ours with lots of sage and giblets. A large Christmas ham covered with pineapple and Maraschino cherries and looking like the cover of a slick magazine for "Christmas Cooking" was our other main meat. We also had an abundance of vegetables from the summer gardens, which had been canned during the summer by Mama Edwards and stored in beautiful glass jars in her pantry. I can hardly write about our Christmas dinner without describing more of the food, such as the giant yeast rolls that only my grandmother could make. With these soft, warm, yummy rolls we ate homemade butter and pears cooked into preserves by my grandmother. I'm not finished yet. We usually had sweet potato pie, fried fruit pies, and sometimes coconut cake made with fresh coconuts from our store. This was all orchestrated by Mama Edwards. This was her Christmas gift to all of us.

The years went by. One by one, cousins would marry, and for a while they would continue to come with their spouses to our Christmas dinners. As they had children, however, they began to make their own new traditions at their homes or with their in-laws. Until my young married days, I continued to join our extended family Christmas dinners and watched as our gatherings morphed with new people coming and others falling off. I too joined this morphing group with my spouse, Ches Danehower. Since my husband and I were from the same area, we could often attend both of our families' Christmas gatherings.

Eventually, Papa Edwards died, and some of our aunts and uncles and even cousins began to pass away. But my grandmother continued on into her eighties, being the glue that held us all together. As Mama Edwards aged, she became unable to do Christmas dinner at her country home in Mandalay; but much to my surprise, my mother stepped up as the annual event's organizer. Mother took on the mantel of cook...with lots of help, of course. One of the last Christmas dinners I remember with all the family present was at my parents' home in Osceola where they then lived (close to both Mandalay and Blytheville). They had purchased and renovated an historic three-story English Tudor house that was set among about five acres of pecan trees. The house was lovely and served as an outlet for my mother's need for a "project."

As Ches and I drove up to the house, I was shocked to see standing prominently in the front window a large aluminum Christmas tree with a fan of lights that rotated colors of red, blue, yellow, and green. I couldn't believe my mother was so modern! Today, when I see one of these old artificial trees in an antique shop, I remember her tree in the window of her English Tudor house and think how, though exceedingly odd, that tree had worked. Perhaps the good cheer and love we always felt for one another allowed everything to work out magically whenever we gathered for our Byrd family Christmas dinners.

VISION OF THE END

❦

Throughout these stories about my young life, our family store is often one of the characters. I think it is only fitting, then, to let you know that the store did not just fade away into history but rather ended in a most dramatic fashion.

In 1955, Byrd's General Store, situated where two gravel roads met in the midst of fields of white gold in Mandalay, Arkansas, lit up the sky with its last gasp of life. But just prior to learning that the store was going up in flames, I had a vision of the end that I am convinced happened. Of all the stories that I've written, this one is the most difficult, because I cannot explain why or how I had this supernatural apparition. Before I recount the event, however, I want to update you on the history of the store before it died.

We had moved to Blytheville in late December of 1944 or early January of 1945, when I was barely six, so it had been years since we had actually lived in Mandalay. Although our new brick store had living quarters built into it, we seldom stayed there. Even though we lived in Blytheville, however, we still had a connection to the store since we "kids" worked there on Saturdays and during the summers. Mother had been the manager of our store for years and continued to be assisted by the capable Mr. Homer and Miss Hollis. As the store business grew, new clerks were hired to help with the growing activity. Daddy would appear now and then to conduct business at the back of the store, and he continued to handle important issues as they arose. He had expanded his cotton business to areas farther south in Arkansas and was often gone for days while clearing additional land to grow cotton. Mother was growing weary of the responsibilities of managing the store, so the time was ripe for change.

I was in my mid-teens in about 1953 when Daddy sold all the contents of the store to Mr. Adams, who wanted to go into the general store business. Daddy would continue to own the store building and the surrounding acreage with the barn, woodshed, and assorted buildings. Mr. Adams would basically be renting the big brick store building from our family.

With our family no longer responsible for the day-to-day operation of the store, we felt released. Still, it was not an easy transition because our lives had always had the store at the center. For example, for the first time in my life to go grocery shopping took extra concentration: I had to remember to make sure I paid for my purchases; I had to watch someone else bag my groceries (they seldom did it correctly in my opinion). And how I missed driving our customers home and the jokes they pulled on me. I now had lots of free time and had to learn how to fill it. Slowly we all began to adjust to our new lifestyle—one that did not include "running" the store.

I was about sixteen years old and into our "new life," when our store came to its fiery end. We were no longer gone from the store; it was gone from us. But what truly makes the end of our store so dramatic was the vision I experienced just prior to learning about the fire. The evening had begun as ordinary as ever at our home in Blytheville. I had gone to bed about 11:00 and was asleep in my room, which was situated on the corner of our house where two streets met. Sometime during the dark night, I was awakened by people who sounded very agitated. Their shouts came from outside our house where the two streets met. I sat up in my bed and tried to focus on the bizarre scene outside my bedroom window taking place in the middle of Holly and Madison Streets. To my surprise there appeared to be a large fire, like a bonfire, with many people standing around it, yelling to one another. My windows were open since the weather was mild, so it seemed odd that there would be a need for a bonfire. It was a strange sight in the middle of the street and in the middle of the night! I continued to rub my eyes and it was difficult to stay awake. I felt that there had to be a logical reason for all of this activity. Possibly, I thought, some pipes had broken or an electrical problem had occurred during the night and workers had come to make repairs. (During the 1950s, smudge pots, a type of lantern using fire, were often placed at construction sites as a warning, so it was not that unusual for me to see fire on streets. Yet the fire I saw through my sleepy eyes seemed way too large to be warning pots.) Unable to focus any longer on this baffling scene, I decided I would check it out in the morning when there would be ample light to see what had happened. I distinctly remember putting my head back on the pillow and falling into a deep sleep immediately.

It was only then, I swear, that the phone rang next to my bed, jarring me out of sleep again. It seemed to me that only minutes had passed since I had fallen back to sleep. On the phone was one of our loyal customers, asking me to alert my parents that our store was burning. Now fully awake and sitting up in my bed, I absorbed the dreadful news. At the same time, I stared out of my windows into a completely silent, pitch-black night. I had never seen such blackness or felt such silence. The fire and the large crowd outside my window had vanished. How could they all have disappeared so quickly?

With confusion and terrible sadness, I got out of bed. I still could not stop staring out of my windows into the dark street. A peculiar feeling enveloped me as I attempted to sort out what I knew I had just seen so clearly; whatever I had experienced was unnatural. All of these thoughts ran through my head as I ran to Mother's room. I told her about the phone call informing us of the terrible news, but I did not mention my mystifying vision. I was still trying to process what had occurred. Daddy was at our other farm, hundreds of miles away in southern Arkansas, so it was Mother who rushed the twenty-four miles to watch helplessly as our store burned to the ground.

When she returned from the horrible disaster, I told my mother about my "vision," not able to think of what else to call it. Until the day she died, Mother always believed I answered the phone about the fire first and then fell asleep for a moment and had "a dream" about it. But I will believe to my dying day that I had a vision that foretold the end of the store. I can never forget the confusion I felt after the call and searching for some evidence to corroborate what I had witnessed.

Over the years I came to accept this experience as one of the mysteries of life. There is nothing I can add or take away from this incident. It is the truth as best I can know and explain it. Today, only trees are growing on the site where our store once stood. The old brick from the store was cleaned and then given to the Avondale Missionary Baptist Church in West Memphis, Arkansas, for a new building. In fact, a hall within the Church was dedicated in 1977 to Daddy for his generosity. The plaque is still on the wall and simply states, "Byrd Hall." So, in a way, Byrd's General Store continues to this day to serve.

THE BLUES, BLADIE MADIE, AND THE LORD

I WAS A SEVEN-YEAR-OLD SECOND GRADER who came home from school one day and found a tall, pretty, twenty-three-year-old black woman with incredible hair, shining eyes, and (though it may be hard to believe I even noticed) beautiful hands. She was talking earnestly with my mother.

Jesse, the wonderful cook of the angel biscuits I described earlier, whom Mother employed when we first moved to Blytheville, had become too ill to continue working. Ruth Jones was recommended for the job as our new housekeeper by her friend, Rosalie, who worked for our neighbor, Mrs. Fleeman. Ruth had been working for a policeman and his family, but they could no longer afford to have help. So Ruth, with good references from the policeman and family, started to work for our family in 1946. She moved into the little white cottage with the Mulberry tree, behind the hedges that grew across our lawn.

This was the simple beginning of Ruth's and my relationship, perhaps as important to me as any I have had with anyone in my life.

At first, when we were all new to each other, Ruth didn't talk very often to any of us. But as months went by, the real Ruth emerged. Let me tell you, she had enough personality and enough confidence to handle my entire extended family! I had no idea then that Ruth would become such a vital part of my family for the rest of her life—and most of mine.

Ruth loved to party on Saturday nights. She lived to sing, dance, and tell stories. But most of all she was the master at organizing our household, and we loved and respected her for her work. Ruth declared early on to Mother that she could not cook (although she later confided in me that she could but just didn't want to). However, over time Ruth often cooked, especially with my older sister, Bob, who enjoyed cooking. She frequently said the only thing she didn't do for our family was chauffeur us around, since she couldn't drive a car. But that wasn't quite true either. For example, if she decided to wash our car, which she sometimes did, she would drive it onto the grassy lawn and then return it to our garage.

My clothes have never (I mean to this day) looked as good as they did when Ruth was cleaning and ironing them. Sometimes I would come home from school and her friend Rosalie would be there as well. They would have two ironing boards set up, ironing clothes for both employers. They would be laughing, gossiping, and sometimes drinking a Country Club malt liquor. (Since my parents didn't have any alcohol in the house, I knew this probably wasn't something my folks would approve, so without Ruth ever asking me not to tell I instinctively knew never to bring up the subject.) The point I did learn from these two vibrant women is how to make work fun. I loved to watch them as they "carried on." I also enjoyed the way they included me in their conversation. They listened to me and I listened to them.

Ruth and I developed our little routines. When I came home from school in the mid-1940s, she and I used to watch the *Lone Ranger*, starring Clayton Moore and Jay Silverheels, on television together (she always saw herself in the role of Tonto). Ruth was similar to my grandmother, Mama Edwards, in getting totally immersed in a show and talking back to the actors on the screen and shouting and laughing and predicting what was going to happen and hugging me when it did.

Another change in our house brought by Ruth was with our music. Music was already eclectic in our house even before she came, but now it was over the top. Mama Edwards had introduced me to bluegrass. My mother enjoyed the classical waltzes of Strauss. My father liked the popular songs of the day. But Ruth had a passion for the Delta Blues—and soon so did I. BB King (whom she declared she knew personally), Little Walter, Muddy Waters, and Ruth's and my all-time favorite, James Brown, were some of the singers we listened to. We must have listened to Brown sing "Please, Please, Please Don't Go" a thousand—no five thousand—times. Ruth and I always had our radio tuned to WDIA in Memphis that played the Blues exclusively. U.S. Route 61, which was known as "the Blues Highway" (and "the Cotton Highway" as well) ran just a few blocks from our home in Blytheville, and Ruth pointed out juke joints all along this corridor where our favorite music could be heard live almost every day. I made good use of this information later in my adult life.

Ruth was an exceptional dancer. In fact, she won Blytheville's street dance contest one year, I think around 1949. My family went down to Ash Street, the center of black culture and commerce in town, to watch her perform and stood clapping to the music as a big crowd surrounded her and her partner. Did they look smart! Ruth had deep waves set in her hair, and she had put on makeup and looked like a movie star. (In fact, if Dionne Warwick had been known at this time, people would have thought they were twins.) Ruth and her partner were dressed just alike: new blue jeans and white starched shirts tucked into their jeans. What really set their matching outfits off, however, was a white handkerchief that hung probably two feet long from each dancer's back pocket. Ruth would have called this "stylin'." She taught me to dance, but I was never as good as she was. As an adult, when she would come to visit me, we continued to dance, and sometimes laugh to keep from crying, to the Delta Blues. I must admit I was an adult before I caught on to the double entendre and innuendo lyrics of many of the songs, for example John Lee Hooker's "Crawling King Snake."

Ruth came from a large African American family and was born and raised in Augusta, Arkansas. She was the youngest of nine children, and her arrival into the world was difficult. In fact, even before she was born her story could have been the lyrics for a Delta Blues song. While Ruth's mother, Ophelia White, was pregnant with Ruth and her twin brother, Rudy, the babies' father drowned while the family was on a picnic. Ruth and Rudy were born prematurely, and Ruth did not thrive well. According to Ruth, she was so tiny that at birth her mother could hold her in the palm of her hand. Due to these medical issues Ruth had seizures her entire life, and although all her siblings were educated, she wasn't allowed to continue school because of her illnesses. But I have to tell you that Ruth was plenty smart and talented and vital. She definitely knew how to count money...and no one could ever cheat her!

In her younger days, before she found the Lord (and our family), Ruth got herself in trouble from time to time. During these "wild" days she always carried what she named "Bladie Madie" with her. Bladie Madie was a bright-yellow switch blade Ruth concealed in her bra. Sometimes, after much pleading from me, she allowed me to hold Bladie and switch it open. I don't know if my sisters and brother were aware of Bladie, since I never discussed this with them. Maybe they also played with the knife and just kept quiet too. Ruth had a tumultuous early life, and for good reason she had learned how to defend herself. As I said, she had reason to sing the Blues. But, when Ruth and Bladie were with me, I felt nothing but loved and protected.

As far as I know, Ruth only used her knife once in a fight.

This was after a Miss Estelle, an "acquaintance," shot her. It seems Miss Estelle had taken a liking to Ruth's husband—and he to her. Ruth had married James Jones on Easter Sunday in about 1951 and was divorced from James on Mother's Day of the same year. Yes, this marriage lasted only a few weeks. But it was not a traditional divorce in a court of law. Here is the story as I heard it years later from Ruth: "When Miss Estelle shot me in the stomach, on Mother's Day no less, I considered that bullet to be James' and my divorce!" Although Ruth was bleeding profusely from the gunshot wound, she took out Bladie Madie and cut Miss Estelle. Ruth said, "I didn't cut Miss Estelle so deep as to kill her, but I cut her everywhere but the bottoms of her feet." The irony here was that James worked at the hospital and was there when his wife and his girlfriend arrived simultaneously in the ER! Both women survived, but Ruth left us for a few months and went to Ypsilanti, Michigan, where she had family, to recover. My parents never discussed this event with us children. Perhaps they needed time to assess the situation. No matter. Ruth returned, and the family once again felt complete. Ruth remained single for the rest of her life.

I don't know for sure if the fight and resulting injury was a turning point in Ruth's religious conversion, but it did happen at some point in her life with us. She now had positive proof of the existence of God. As an example of her belief, she had been a heavy smoker and prayed this addiction would be taken from her. And it was: She was unable to smoke a cigarette without becoming physically ill; the cure was immediate and, as far as Ruth was concerned, an answer to her prayers. As she grew older, she maintained her upbeat personality, but with God in her life she definitely changed. She was now slow to anger and was thoughtful to those in need. My older sister, Bob, gave Ruth the Bible on tape and this proved to be one of Ruth's most meaningful possessions. Ruth seemed to have memorized the whole Bible by listening to those tapes. If she felt I needed to be reprimanded about something, she found a creative way to admonish me: When I was out of the house, she would call and leave an appropriate Bible verse on my answering machine. Sometimes I would think, that isn't in the Bible, but I would look up the verse and I never found her to be wrong. And she was right (and helpful) in pointing out my shortcomings. Ruth had committed her life to our family, and we had committed ours to her. When she passed away in 2002, I was honored to be the one asked to give her eulogy at her funeral. So, to end my story about Ruth, here is some of what I said:

> *Ruth came into our lives when we were small children. Her life was woven with ours for almost sixty years. She gave us laughter, unconditional love, and a spirit for the Lord. After Ruth arrived, our lives were never the same. She made sure we didn't dance like "white folks," that we heard the music she liked and could rhyme our words when we talked. She made the ordinary day-to-day events fun and special. In fact, she made each child*

she dealt with feel important, needed, and loved. As we grew up, Ruth's heart grew too. She loved our children as if they were her own grandchildren, and their children as if they were her own great-grandchildren. When any of us needed her, she was there, and she always gave more than she took. Somewhere along the way, Ruth became a prayer warrior. In her later years, she and her friends from her church formed a "prayer band." They spent hours in prayer for us, our friends, and their family and friends. Ruth often sang sweet songs with her beautiful voice. Although as she grew older her voice would crack, the words were always uplifting. Some of her favorite sayings were: "Keep your eyes on the cross;" "God doesn't always come when you wants, but He always comes on time;" and "The Lord willing." Ruth loved us, and we loved Ruth. In thinking about her today, I can't help but to be reminded of Ruth in the Bible. Ruth 1:16-17 says, "Entreat me not to leave you or to turn back from following after you; for wherever you go, I will go; and wherever you lodge, I will lodge; your people shall be my people, and your God my God. Where you die, I will die, and there I will be buried."

It is amazing to me every time I realize how Ruth's life seemed to parallel this passage from the Book of Ruth. Like the Ruth of the Bible, our Ruth went wherever we went, lived where we lived, made my family her family, and shared with us her belief in God. She now lies next to the graves of my daddy, George; my mother, Donye; my brother, Don; and my younger sister, Sue. Their final resting place is not far from Highway 61, the corridor of the Delta Blues, in northeastern Arkansas, in a little piece of Earth that is also a little corner of Heaven.

THE WEIRDEST TALE OF ALL

✣

ALL THE STORIES I'VE TOLD YOU IN THIS BOOK are true stories of my childhood. Although this final tale seems to be about my husband as a child—this tale is also about me as a child—as you'll see.

When Ches was a little boy of about ten years old in 1947, his friend, Bopper (I could *not* make this name up), told him about a bobcat that was for sale for five dollars. It seemed that the cat's mother had been killed on White River in Arkansas and left two little orphaned cubs. One cub had sold, and the other was waiting for a home. When Ches asked his father, Big Chester, if he could have five dollars to buy the cub, without hesitation Big Chester said, "Sure, we'll try to mate the bobcat with a Persian and start a new breed." (I have always hoped this was a joke, but who knows?) The little bobcat was named Kid Bob, and he had the run of the Danehower house. Like all wild animals, he (I mean the bobcat) was wild. Ches and Kid Bob enjoyed their life together. In fact, they had fifteen minutes of fame when they appeared together in the magazine *The Arkansas Sportsman* in 1947.

To this day, my husband keeps a picture of himself holding

Kid Bob on his desk—right next to a picture of me. (I'm not sure which is more precious to him.) As I might have mentioned, Kid Bob was wild, and Ches' arms bore deeper and deeper scratches as time went by. Gurrie, Ches' mother, wore the same telltale signs on her legs.

The final episode that caused Kid Bob to become an orphan again was when he jumped on a table with an open bottle of ink sitting on it. The ink became airborne and hit the wall with a big splat against newly hung wallpaper. Enough said about that! The bobcat was banished by Ches' father to go live inside a cotton gin in Blytheville and be its guard cat. Now this plan for Kid Bob still sounds suspicious to me. It reminds me of the plan to mate Kid Bob with a Persian cat and create a new breed.

Ches visited Kid Bob once at the cotton gin and found the bobcat had gotten quite large and seemed calmed because he had probably been neutered. That was the last time Ches saw Kid Bob. He was told about two months later that the bobcat had died.

Flash forward over forty years. I had heard this crazy tale of Kid Bob many (I mean too many) times. Then one day (mind you, I had been married to Ches for years by then) the conversation went like this. I said, "You know Ches, I'm not sure why I never thought to tell you about the bobcat our family had." He said, "Your family had a bobcat?" I replied, "Well yes, but it wasn't part of our family like Kid Bob. In fact, it wasn't even alive. It had been stuffed by a taxidermist and my daddy bought it somewhere and brought it home. Mother found it creepy to have a dead bobcat sitting on Daddy's desk at home, so she threw it into the back of a closet."

"Where did your father get it?" Ches asked.

"I don't know, Daddy was always bringing strange things home that he would find here and there. He said he got the stuffed bobcat at...Oh my gosh, Ches...he said he got it from a cotton gin!"

After all these years I had never put two and two together. My husband and I compared our notes and the timeline during the saga of Kid Bob and the acquisition of our stuffed bobcat. Ches and I had lived about fifteen miles apart, but in different towns of Mississippi County, Arkansas. Both our fathers did business with cotton gins in the surrounding area. So, it fit perfectly: Kid Bob ended up in my house, or should I say closet.

Didn't I tell you that this was the weirdest tale of all? Therefore, I am going to end this book with it. Kid Bob lives on.

APPENDICES

THE DITCHES*

It was impossible for me to write my stories and not mention the ditches, since our very existence depended on this ditch and drainage system that surrounded us. Some of the ditches are what you would normally think of as a ditch, but the "numbered" ditches I mention in my stories were more like canals. Today the levees, ditches and pumping stations have continued to improve, thus keeping the crops and people safe.

I vividly remember riding with my parents in the 1940s between Blytheville and Mandalay and observing the Big Lake area. It was like a huge wild river with many whirlpools and fast-moving water over rocks and around trees. Sometimes we drove through water-covered roads when a weak place in a levee would fail or there was too much rain and there was nowhere for the water to drain. Little River, which is actually a tributary of the St. Francis River, ran into Big Lake just at the Missouri border near the town of Manila.

Somehow, the lake and tributary were harnessed, and now peaceful lily pads cover the area that once wildly churned. It is a

---

* The scientific information that I have included about the ditches, drainage, floods, earthquakes, swamp areas, and government projects was gathered from the Encyclopedia of Arkansas History and Culture. Their computer site is a compilation of research by hundreds of scholars who have studied these topics.

protected area known as the Big Lake National Wildlife Refuge, located two miles from Manila. State Road 77, which we traveled from Manila to State Road 158 where our house-store stood, is now a smooth highway perched along the top of a great levee. From the top of this levee highway, one can look out over the flat, magnificent landscape and see the rich fertile land that defines the Arkansas Delta of Mississippi County and our little settlement of Mandalay.

Before you can understand the importance of the ditching and drainage of the land in Mississippi County, you have to look at its geographical location and history. The county is named after the Mississippi River that defines its eastern border and is located on the dangerous New Madrid fault. Growing up on this fault, we became accustomed to small tremors that seemed to occur quite often with little notice or fanfare. In the massive earthquakes of 1811 and 1812, however, the Mississippi River flowed backwards, creating lakes and upheavals in Northeast Arkansas and Southeast Missouri.

When Hernando de Soto, the famous Spanish explorer, crossed the Mississippi River in 1541, the exact path he took is not precisely known, but it is believed he visited parts of Mississippi County. De Soto's party described a big lake that existed on a high, dry area near the Mississippi River and a feeding moat around a large village believed to be in the area of contemporary Gosnell, Mississippi County. According to scholars the lake was actually moved by a catastrophic earthquake, creating an 11,000-acre lake aptly named "Big Lake" near Manila in Mississippi County. Prior to becoming Big Lake, it was part of the Mississippi River; but now the Mississippi River lies about twenty-five miles to the lake's east. In addition to the lake's being reconfigured, what was called Buffalo Island (Island in metaphor only) where thousands of buffalo roamed in the western part of Mississippi County, sank. No wonder this area was called the "Great Swamp" on early Arkansas maps. This swamp ran from the Mississippi River on the east to the St. Francis River "Sunken Lands" on the west.

In 1859, Mississippi County's western border was changed, and Craighead County was formed, so the Buffalo Island area was divided between the two counties. In 1879, Congress created the Mississippi River Commission to allow a united flood-control plan under the administration of the U.S. Army Corps of Engineers. Between 1905 and 1915, the Arkansas General Assembly passed laws to create a program of flood controls in the Arkansas River Valley. Mississippi County then became part of the St. Francis Levee/Drainage District.

At that time only five percent of Mississippi County's land was cultivated, and only another five percent was deemed capable of cultivation. Ninety percent of the land was regarded as a hopelessly permanent mosquito-and-malaria-infested swamp. After years of building levees and draining the swamp, however, railroads came in and timber was clear cut. In fact, lumbering became a huge industry in the first quarter of the twentieth century, with as many as thirty-five sawmills in Mississippi County.

Then the great flood of 1927 hit. It was one of the most destructive in the history of the United States, and for Arkansas it was the most costly flood in its history. Measures were strengthened and increased after this flood, prompting the Flood Control Act of 1928. Then came the flood of 1937, with a cold, rainy January setting the stage. The Mississippi River levees that had been built since the 1927 flood did not break, but all the Arkansas waterways overflowed, inundating or affecting seventeen counties, flooding about 1,800,000 acres of land. Diversion ditches were built somewhat parallel to the St. Francis River to serve as an outlet for excess water in times of floods. The Army Corps of Engineers installed the world's largest siphons on the St. Francis River in 1939 to help with flood control. And in 1977, the U.S. Corps of Engineers built the W.G. Huxtable Pumping Plant in Lee County to prevent the Mississippi River floodwater from moving into the St. Francis. It is considered the world's largest pumping plant of its kind.

The Mississippi Alluvial Plain, aka "the Arkansas Delta," on which Mandalay is situated is a distinctive natural region because of its flat surface and the flow of its large streams. The built-up layers of deep soil, gravel, and clay transported from the Rockies to the west and Appalachians to the east have resulted in a terrain and soil suitable for large-scale farming. In fact, the Mississippi Alluvial Plain (created by the Mississippi River) is one of the most agriculturally productive regions in the world. Mississippi County was once the world's largest producer of rain-grown cotton—the "fields of white gold" from my childhood.

THE INDIAN MOUND[*]

When I walked about a mile from my house on Holly Street in Blytheville to the far end of the street, I could see what we called simply "the Indian Mound" sitting in a field about one or two miles away. I have gone back as an adult to see it, and I'm shocked to see how badly it has been eroded by the weather and perhaps people digging there. It seems to me to be half the size it was in the 1940s.

When I was about eleven or twelve years old, a group of my neighborhood friends and I decided to walk to the mound to picnic. It was a hot day and once there we saw that holes had been dug all over the mound, giving it the appearance of pockmarks. Small trees, underbrush of wild bushes, and weeds covered the site, making it most unpleasant for picnicking. I don't recall any signs saying it was off limits, but if there had been we probably would have chosen not to notice them.

This mound, referred to as the "Chickasawba" or "Blytheville" Mound, was studied in 1894 by Cyrus Thomas when he explored the question of the origin of the Native American mound builders for the United Stated Bureau of American Ethnology. However, it was 1984 before the Mound was finally protected by being listed in the National Register of Historic Places as an "archeological site" (3M55).

---

[*] The Encyclopedia of Arkansas History and Culture *provided archeological information that is included in this narrative.*

In my research to learn more about the Chickasawba Mound, I could not find a definitive answer regarding the purpose of this particular mound. *The Encyclopedia of Arkansas History and Culture* seems to give the best answer about these human constructs in general: "Indian Mounds were constructed by deliberately heaping soil, rock, or other material (such as ash, shell, and the remains of burned buildings) onto natural land surfaces. In Arkansas, Native Americans built earthen mounds for ritual or burial purposes or as the location for important structures, but mound-building ceased shortly after European contact, due to changes in religious and other cultural practices. Mississippian people in eastern Arkansas were using mounds when Spanish explorers arrived in 1541. Most of the thousands of mounds built in Arkansas have been destroyed by modern development and vandalism, but several hundred remain. Today, they are recognized as important religious and cultural monuments."

It is impossible for me to write about the Blytheville Mound without discussing the exciting new information I learned about the Native Americans who lived in this area. Within a "stone's throw" of this mound is the air base that I wrote about in "The Biggest Worry of All." Prior to the base's closing in 1992, the base was approved in the early 1950s as a Strategic Air Command. In 1988, the base was renamed Eaker Air Force Base in honor of World War II Commander of the Eighth Air Force, General Ira C. Eaker. He was awarded a Congressional Gold Medal for his contribution to the development of aviation and the security of his country. When the base closed, Jimmy McNeil of the Memphis District of the U.S. Army of Engineers suggested that the site be removed from cultivation in order to preserve any remaining archeological items. In 1996, the Eaker Site was declared a National Historic Landmark and is on the National Register of Historic Places (3MS105).

The Eaker Site, named after the base, is considered the largest and most intact Late Mississippian Nodena site in the Central Mississippi Valley. The site, like most Mississippian settlements, stands on the bank of a river, in this case the Pemiscot Bayou, which was a major waterway in earlier times. Again, according to the *Encyclopedia of Arkansas,* "Archeologists use the term 'Nodena' to describe the Native American way of life along the Mississippi River that the Eaker Site represents. The site is believed to have been a Nodena-Phase town, with sturdy permanent houses, a defensive wall and ditch, and a mound." The site had three archeological periods: Late Woodland about 600 AD, Late Mississippian about 1250 AD, and the Late Mississippian Nodena Phase about 1350-1450 AD. Historians believe that this is possibly the village that Spanish explorer Hernando de Soto visited in the 1540s. With only 5.5% of survey mapping completed, eighty underground man-made anomalies have already been identified. Archaeologists estimate that perhaps 400 prehistoric homes may be buried at the site.

In all my years of growing up so close to this mound, I never considered the settlements that were built around it. It is exciting for me to know that some research has been done discovering the homes of the original settlers. Although research has now ceased at the Eaker Site; it is there waiting for the scientists to return.

THE BLUES

I AM NO AUTHORITY ON THE DELTA BLUES, but I know what I like.

I also like what Charlie Musselwhite, internationally known blues musician, said when he compared country music and the blues. He said that a country guy might sing, "My baby left me, I'm going to go jump off a bridge," but a blues guy would sing, "My baby left me, I'm gonna find me a new baby." Blues music was born in the Mississippi Delta. This is Mississippi, Tennessee, and Arkansas. B.B. King made me laugh with his comment on the "real" home of the blues. He said, "When I first came to Memphis, it was back in '46. We would have a little thing down on Beale Street. At that time, they called Memphis the home of the blues. Then Chicago took it, and I got mad. I been mad ever since. The home of the blues is not Chicago. It's Memphis!"

Many blues musicians lived in Mississippi County, and particularly in the town of Osceola, so they usually found their way to Memphis only fifty miles away. In Osceola, they celebrate these musicians with historic plaques on Main Street. In honor of these talented men here is what is written:

Willie Bloom: *Osceola's own "Sweet Man." Willie Bloom captured Southern cotton workers' sentiment with his* legendary Blues music dating back to 1918. Bloom, whose recordings included "Osceola Blues," played alongside musical giants such as W.C. Handy, Jimmy Lunceford, Fats Pichon, Louis Armstrong, Count Basie, and Fats Waller.

Albert King: *Moving to Osceola with his family at age eight, blues legend Albert King (1923-1992) earned an early living picking cotton on nearby farms. King began his magnificent professional career in Osceola with his group, In the Groove Boys. King's T99 Club, once located here, hosted musical icons traveling between St. Louis and Memphis.*

Billy Lee Riley: *Began picking cotton at age seven on the Jacksonville plantation in Osceola. Influenced by local bluesmen, Riley (1933-2009) became a 1950s rockabilly star, recording his first hit, "Flying Saucers Rock & Roll," at Sun Studios. Retiring from music after performing worldwide, Riley was coaxed out of retirement by Bob Dylan in 1992.*

Son Seals: *Osceola native Frank "Son" Seals (1942-2004) began playing professionally at thirteen with Robert Nighthawk, then formed his own band at seventeen, touring with Albert King. Winner of three W.C. Handy Awards for best Blues recording of the year, Seals' riveting guitar riffs made him a perennial favorite along the Cotton Highway.*

Jimmy "Popeye" Thomas: *Osceola's native Jimmy Thomas split his youth working in local cotton fields and playing in local juke joints. As a teenager, he joined Ike Turner's Kings of Rhythm group as lead singer, later performing with the Ike and Tina Turner Review. Settling in London, England, in 1969, Thomas launched the Osceola Records production studio.*

Reggie Young: *Called the most prolific session guitarist of all time, Reggie Young (1936-2019) grew up along the Cotton Highway in Osceola in the 1940s. He played with a multitude of famous artists, including Johnny Cash, Elvis Presley, the Beatles, and Willie Nelson. Young has performed all types of music, including many songs dealing with his cotton heritage.*

Nowadays people in other places the world over play and sing the blues. And why not?

Interest seems to be growing in knowing more about this genre of music. Mississippi has museums specifically dedicated to the blues. Clarksdale has the Delta Blues Museum, and Indianola has the B.B. King and Delta Interpretive Center. I'm sure there are many more, and with a little research you can find them.

THE (INFAMOUS) $100.00 CAKE RECIPE FROM OPAL WOODS AND THE WALDORF ASTORIA

CAKE

1 cup butter (room temperature)

2½ cups of sugar

5 eggs (separate yolks and whites)

3 cups plain flour

4 (rounded) teaspoons cocoa

1 teaspoon soda

pinch salt

1 cup buttermilk

5 tablespoons strong, brewed coffee

2 teaspoons vanilla

Combine butter and sugar and blend thoroughly. Beat egg yolks and add to sugar and butter mixture. Mix well. Sift dry ingredients together. Set aside. Beat egg whites until stiff. Set aside. Mix remaining liquids together. Set aside. Alternate the dry and liquid ingredients into the butter, sugar, and yolk mixture. When this is well mixed, fold in well-beaten egg whites.

Pour into three butter-and-flour-dusted cake pans and bake in pre-heated 375-degree oven for 30 minutes or until done. Do not overcook, cake will be too dry.

ICING

1 16-oz. box powdered sugar
3 teaspoons cocoa
1 stick butter (room temperature)
1 teaspoon vanilla
3 tablespoons strong, brewed coffee

Sift sugar with cocoa. Cream butter and add sugar, cocoa, and liquids. Beat well. Spread between layers and on cake. I often double the icing recipe since our family prefers more icing.

OPTIONAL

The original recipe adds a raw egg yolk to the icing. I don't do this, but I do add additional coffee and butter to increase the needed liquid.

TWO FAMOUS OPPOSITES
FROM MISSISSIPPI COUNTY

THERE ARE A FEW MOVIE STARS, SINGERS, AND WRITERS who have some connection to Mississippi County, Arkansas, including actresses Julie Adams and Dale Evans and even writer John Grisham, whose grandfather owned a music store in Blytheville. Their stories are not found here. But there are two men who have a connection with Blytheville that I just have to mention.

Johnny Cash, although born in Cleveland County, Arkansas, came to the Dyess Colony in Mississippi County when he was three years old. This Colony represented Roosevelt's attempt at American socialism (this story is for another day). Anyway, Johnny Cash needs no introduction from me. He first sang on the radio at station KLCN in Blytheville while attending Dyess High School, which lies about twenty-five or thirty miles outside Blytheville. This performance was prior to his graduation in 1950. Of course, we all know he became a world-renowned singer/songwriter of country and gospel music. The "man in black" and all of that!

Okay, not to cause major shock here, but who do you think might be the antithesis of Johnny Cash?

Would you suspect the forever tan, dapper-dressing movie star George Hamilton? Yes, it is true. I know for sure, since George attended Blytheville Central Grade School with me for a few years. His family lived with his mother's parents in a lovely house on Main Street (the same Main Street that I wrote about in my stories) in Blytheville. George did not reside very long in Blytheville. In his book *Don't Mind If I Do,* George describes Blytheville quite well. I was surprised he confessed to his Blytheville roots, since I once saw an interview with him where he said he was from Memphis.

I must add a note here that if you are under forty years of age, you may not even remember George Hamilton. But I'll bet you still listen to Johnny Cash!

ACKNOWLEDGMENTS

The first person I want to acknowledge is my editor and publisher, Greg Pierce of ACTA Publications, Chicago, Illinois. He has my enduring gratitude for taking a chance on a writer with her first book. My work is better because of the challenges Greg gave me to dig a little deeper. I believe our common values of wanting the world to be a better place, loving our families, and sharing our faith united us in the process.

The idea for writing my stories began simply enough. At a holiday luncheon my host and artist friend, Marlene Miller, suggested her guests tell something about the circumstances of their births. When it was my turn, I said I was born in the middle of a cotton field, and then the questions began! I am thankful Marlene (although unknowingly) motivated me to write down my stories.

I finished a few of them and read them to my three daughters, Dana Baldwin, Georgie Kastelic, and Lane Muzzarelli (and her husband, Bill). Getting a positive nod from them, I then moved to a tougher audience—my grandchildren—and even they approved and asked for more.

I thank my lifelong Arkansas friends for allowing me to write about them and/or encouraging me to complete the stories. I used their maiden names in the stories since that was how I first knew them. These "girls" include: Gail Brogdon, Sally McCutchen, Nelia Woods, and Barbara Dale Dunlap. Then, there is my special Arkansas friend and the first editor of my stories, Cookie (Glenda Lee Poetz) Coppedge. She is a retired instructor of English at Arkansas State University. Since Cookie and I have a shared history together, she was able to make great suggestions to improve the continuity of the book. I am grateful for her good eye, knowledge of English, and passion for seeing the stories in print.

My Chicago friends, the artist ISz and his wife, Mary Rickey-Struben, loved my stories from the beginning and offered to help with my book project. ISz, an accomplished visual artist, agreed to design a cover that reflects his nontraditional vision of cotton fields. In some ways my stories are not traditional; therefore, I feel his art perfectly complements my narratives.

My sister, Bobbie Jean (Bob), was most helpful when I needed confirmation of dates for events I wrote about in the book, and I am very appreciative of my husband, Ches, for his interest and encouragement.

Finally, thanks to Ke Francis, writer and artist who shares southern cotton roots with me, for his kind comments about my book. And early on in the writing of my stories, Mary Gay Shipley, who is a legend in the art and history of the Arkansas Delta, encouraged my writing. I am deeply appreciative to both of them for their comments that appear on the back cover.

ABOUT THE AUTHOR AND THE ARTIST

GEORGE ANN BYRD DANEHOWER is a museum educator, university art gallery director, and artist. She has served as a panelist reviewing grants for the Illinois Arts Council and was the recipient of two Kellogg Foundation Fellowship Workshop scholarships to study at the Field Museum in Chicago, Illinois. She attended art history classes at the Prado in Madrid, Spain, and graduated from Bradley University in Peoria, Illinois. Prior to *Fields of White Gold*, she focused her writing on projects within a museum or university setting: catalogs about artists and exhibitions, childrens' guides, and other educational materials. This is her first book of stories based on her life experiences.

George Ann has lived in Spain, New Orleans, Denver, San Antonio, and the Washington D.C. area. Her husband Ches Danehower is a retired dermatologist, and the couple have three daughters and six grandchildren. They live most of the year in Peoria, Illinois, but spend the winter in New Orleans, the Gulf Coast, and North Carolina.

ISz is a Chicago-based artist whose work creates Oneness. He has illustrated several books for ACTA Publications, including *The Baby in Mommy's Tummy, How to Avoid Burnout, An A-Z Guide to Letting Go, Page the Poet, In the Beginning,* and *We the (little) People* (a collection of 50 of his black-and-white, pen-and-ink drawings suitable for framing). His substantial body of art—including prints, paintings, and other media—can be viewed at www.iszartstudio.com.

If you search today for the Mandalay I have written about, you will find this sign. Most of the people are gone, as well as the busy corner of commerce that was our family's home-store. The fields of cotton that dazzled my eyes as I looked in every direction remain now mostly as memories in my mind. I hope this book will help you remember the fields of white gold in your own life.

GEORGE ANN BYRD DANEHOWER